Victorious SPIRITUAL WARFARE

MARILYN HICKEY

LEGACY
PUBLISHERS INTERNATIONAL

VICTORIOUS SPIRITUAL WARFARE
ISBN 1-880809-44-3

Copyright © 2005 by Marilyn Hickey
P. O. Box 17340
Denver, CO 80217

Published by Legacy Publishers, Inc.
1301 South Clinton Street
Denver, Colorado 80247-2329

1 2 3 4 5 6 7 8 9 10 / 09 08 07 06 05

Contents

Introduction

Too many people today are struggling over prolonged situations that drain them of their energy and faith. We need to realize that we are not fighting a *natural* battle—we are in *spiritual warfare!*

Spiritual warfare requires a supernatural plan of attack, using supernatural weapons, applying supernatural methods, and releasing supernatural ability. When we use God's weapons and His way, we win!

That's why I've written this book. You cannot afford to be ignorant of Satan's devices. I want you to know the truth about his work, his army, and how to resist him. Just as there is an hierarchy in the U.S. Army, there is a rank and file in Satan's army. You need to understand this hierarchy, and how they maneuver and gain entrance into your life and circumstances.

In the beginning, Satan (Lucifer) was glorious to behold, created by God as an angel of praise. However, he tried to take God's throne and lost God's glory. Since then, the devil has dedicated himself to opposing God. He tempts us to sin, then casts blame on our character.

The devil also casts doubt on who God is, and he aims at pulling down the kingdom of God. The devil has no compassion. His power is used only for evil, to destroy everything good. He destroys in order to show his own power.

It is important to remember, however, that the devil is not all-powerful.

For every move that the devil makes, God has a countermove. For every power play, maneuver, strategy, or evil attack that Satan may attempt to launch against you, God has given you a counterattack that will put the devil on his back and his demon powers fleeing from you in fear.

The devil may have declared war on you, as a believer, but you are about to become armed and dangerous (with Word-based knowledge and understanding of your spiritual weapons). I believe that by the time you finish reading this book, you will be changed into what I call a "Satan-proofer"—someone who transforms the circumstances around them—and receive the victory God has promised in His Word.

The most important thing you can remember is that you are a child of God and are protected from the wiles of the enemy. God told you that because He loves you, "No weapon that is formed against thee shall prosper.... This is the heritage of the servants of the LORD, and their righteousness is of me, saith the LORD" (Isaiah 54:17). Praise God! You are the victor!

CHAPTER 1

Know Your Foe!

A good soldier would never enter into battle without first studying his opponent. He wouldn't carry a bow and arrow onto the battlefield if his enemy had guns. And he certainly wouldn't ignore a declaration of war, choosing to believe his enemy didn't exist, thereby leaving himself defenseless against a powerful, destructive force.

The devil has declared war, and you are his target. He knows your weaknesses, and he will take every advantage to defeat you. However, in this war, he is the one carrying the bow and arrows; and you have been given the superior "firepower." You are guaranteed victory; he is guaranteed eternal defeat. You never have to lose another battle with the devil again! It's time you learned about your enemy and how to use your spiritual weapons. It's time to fight back.

Lucifer, the angel Satan, has not always been the archenemy of God. In fact, Satan's beginnings were marvelous and beautiful. He lived in heaven and his name was "...Lucifer, son of the morning!..." (Isaiah 14:12). He dwelt in the presence of God, covering His throne with his wings. In fact, he was so special that God called him His "anointed cherub" (Ezekiel 28:14).

He was a cherub, but he wasn't a "cupid"—a chubby baby with wings and an arrow to pierce someone's heart. He was a big, powerful, important angel.

1

Cherubim are first mentioned in the Bible when God sent two to guard the entrance of the Garden of Eden after Adam and Eve fell:

> *...he placed at the east of the garden of Eden Cherubims, and a flaming sword which turned every way, to keep the way of the tree of life.*

> Genesis 3:24

We see from their duty east of Eden that cherubim are strong, fighting angels who are given extremely significant responsibilities. Because of their position, God always puts them in pairs. Two cherubim guarded the Mercy Seat that covered the Ark of the Covenant:

> *And thou shalt make two cherubims of gold, of beaten work shalt thou make them, in the two ends of the mercy seat. And the cherubims shall stretch forth their wings on high, covering the mercy seat with their wings, and their faces shall look one to another....*

> Exodus 25:18,20

This Mercy Seat is a replica of the one in heaven's temple (Hebrews 8:2-3). So in heaven, two real cherubim cover the eternal Mercy Seat, the place where God meets with His people and communes with them (Exodus 25:22). The cherubim protect the holiness of God and they fellowship with Him.

Lucifer enjoyed all these rights and responsibilities in heaven before his fall. Imagine, he celebrated God's presence and, alone, he covered God's throne with his wings!

Lucifer's Rise and Fall

I believe Lucifer was one of three archangels, together with Gabriel and Michael. *Arch* means "chief," so these three angels commanded the angelic hosts. They were in charge of three areas: Gabriel was the chief messenger angel; Michael was the chief warrior; and Lucifer was the worship leader. Each archangel commanded a third of all the angels.

As an archangel, Lucifer led worship and praise of God. His voice was so beautiful it was almost indescribable. It sounded like he had a whole orchestra built inside of him, and his praise was more soothing and exhilarating and moving than any concert or symphony. He literally covered God's throne with praise.

Lucifer not only sang like an angel, but he also performed music on instruments with great ability and grace: "...the workmanship of thy tabrets [tambourines] and of thy pipes [such as flutes, clarinets, and oboes] was prepared in thee in the day that thou wast created" (Ezekiel 28:13).

Lucifer was gorgeous in appearance. The Lord gave the prophet Ezekiel a vision of Satan's former glory:

> ...*Thou sealest up the sum, full of wisdom, and perfect in beauty. Thou hast been in Eden the garden of God; every precious stone was thy covering, the sardius* [ruby], *topaz, and the diamond, the beryl* [a rare metal that ranges in color from bluish green to yellow, white, pink, and deep green], *the onyx* [a black and white striped quartz], *and the jasper* [a polished reddish, brown or yellow quartz], *the sapphire, the emerald, and the carbuncle* [a gem similar to turquoise], *and gold:... Thou wast perfect in thy ways from the day that thou wast created, till iniquity was found in thee.*

> Ezekiel 28:12-13,15

Lucifer's body glistened with the sparkling, colorful jewels and metals. However, the sight of his splendor did not turn Lucifer's heart toward God in praise; instead, the sight of his beauty swelled his chest with rebellious pride. Lucifer believed that the gift of his beauty entitled him to be equal with Almighty God, not thankful to Him (Ezekiel 28:15).

I believe Lucifer's fall was not that different from Adam and Eve's. God made Adam and Eve for fellowship and praise. They were happy and joyful in the Garden of Eden until they chose to believe the lie of the devil instead of God's own truth.

Satan, too, was created for fellowship and worship, but he chose to believe the lie of his own pride and greed. God didn't create Adam, Eve, or Satan to be evil, but He did give them a free will. He allowed them to choose between righteousness and wickedness, but all three chose wrongly.

Lucifer's problem began when he wanted the angels to worship him rather than God. He tried to exalt himself. But God would not stand for anyone worshiping anyone or anything other than Himself:

For thou [Lucifer] *hast said in thine heart, I will ascend into heaven, I will exalt my throne above the stars of God: I will sit also upon the mount of the congregation, in the sides of the north: I will ascend above the heights of the clouds; I will be like the most High.*

Isaiah 14:13-14

These five statements, which I call the five "I Wills," eloquently define who Satan is. He wants to be like God because he thinks God is power. God is not power, He is love and mercy.

Lucifer's "I Will" statements came directly from his heart (Matthew 12:34), and the Word says that out of the heart comes "...the issues of life" (Proverbs 4:23). What was in Lucifer's heart? Pride. Willfulness. Lust for power. Although he was very brilliant, beautiful, and musical, Lucifer's pride and lusts made him ugly and unacceptable to God.

Pride led to his fall: "Pride goeth before destruction, and an haughty spirit before a fall" (Proverbs 16:18). In his pride, Lucifer set himself up as a god before the Father. He worshiped the idol of his own beauty.

Lucifer's attitude made him a loser. God had to cast him from heaven because He "...resisteth the proud..." (1 Peter 5:5) and He does not find "...pleasure in wickedness: neither shall evil dwell with [God]" (Psalm 5:4).

How art thou fallen from heaven, O Lucifer, son of the morning! how art thou cut down to the ground, which didst weaken the nations! Yet thou shalt be brought down to hell, to the sides of the pit.

Isaiah 14:12,15

Being cast out of heaven was not the only consequence of Lucifer's sins. He was punished in three ways. The first punishment occurred in Eden after he caused Adam and Eve to sin:

*And the LORD God said unto the serpent, Because thou hast done this,
thou art cursed above all cattle, and above every beast of the field; upon
thy belly shalt thou go, and dust shalt thou eat all the days of thy life: And
I will put enmity between thee and the woman, and between thy seed and
her seed; it shall bruise thy head, and thou shalt bruise his heel.*

Genesis 3:14-15

God then judged Satan at the Cross. When you came to the Cross and took Jesus into your heart, you were given authority over the devil and set free from his clutches—free from sin and its penalty of death and hell. The devil was defeated by Christ's actions on the Cross. The final judgment will be when God casts the devil from the earth into the Lake of Fire, where he will burn for all time: "And the devil that deceived them was cast into the lake of fire and brimstone... and shall be tormented day and night for ever and ever" (Revelation 20:10).

Authority to Overcome

Lucifer did not take the humiliation of losing his place and authority lying down. If he was going to be kicked out of paradise, he was going to take as many of God's angels with him as he could. As he exited his heavenly home, Lucifer swept a third of the angels down to earth, to roam with him and oppress God's creation:

*And there appeared another wonder in heaven; and behold a great red
dragon, having seven heads and ten horns, and seven crowns upon his
heads. And his tail drew the third part of the stars of heaven, and did cast
them to the earth.... And the great dragon was cast out, that old serpent,
called the Devil, and Satan, which deceiveth the whole world...*

Revelation 12:3,4,9

While on earth, he does his best to terrify man, stalking his prey and roaring the way a lion would: "...your adversary the devil, as a roaring lion, walketh about, seeking whom he may devour" (1 Peter 5:8).

Notice, God didn't say the devil is a lion; Satan just pretends to be a lion. He is always trying to counterfeit God and His power. The real Lion is Jesus! He's the Lion of the tribe of Judah (Revelation 5:5), and when you are born again, you receive this Lion nature in your life. You have the power, strength, and authority of Jesus inside you.

I remember a time when a young girl came forward after a church service to have a counselor pray for her. She was oppressed by demons and was seeking the prayers of a Christian to be set free. Several Christians and I gathered around her and began to rebuke the demons, but the girl wasn't getting any better. I got down next to her ear and quietly said to the girl, "You tell the demons to go in Jesus' name." She said, "I can't!" I told her that she could, but she said, "I can't!"

I asked her if she was born again and she said, "Yes." I told her that, because she was a Christian, if she was sincere, she could get rid of the demons attacking her. So she said, "Go! In Jesus' name! Within a split second, that girl was changed. I've never seen anyone change so quickly—she was transformed.

She came to me later and said that although she was a Christian, she had been getting into the occult and demonism. As a result, demons had begun to attack and oppress her. She didn't know what authority she had in the name of Jesus, so she kept turning to Christians to pray for her release from the demons.

Every time she would be set free, however, they would return because she did not know her kingdom authority. Now, with the realization of her God-given dominion over the devil and his demons, she is able to overcome him whenever she feels him coming against her. You, too, have the authority to overcome the devil and his demons. Whenever you hear Satan roaring in your ear, tempting you to sin or attempting to frighten you with his threats of destruction, all you have to do is say, "Get out in Jesus' name! " Resist the devil. Not only will he get away from you, the Bible says that he will flee from you! (See James 4:7.) Praise God.

Portrait of the Enemy

Satan's entire character can be summed up with three words: thief, murderer, and destroyer. Everything he wants, everything he does, is to achieve these three goals. He only wants to do evil!

The book of Job is an excellent place to see Satan's threefold nature. He killed Job's children and servants; destroyed his animals, crops, and property, and stole Job's wealth and health (see Job 1-2). Let's look at some of his other characteristics.

What Satan Believes

Satan believes in continual rebellion against God and anything godly. He will do everything he can, move people in any way necessary, to break up the things of God—life, love, family, church, and government.

Abortion comes from the devil because it is rebellion against what is godly—it is the destruction of life, hope, and peace of mind. The devil causes children to be born without fathers—this break-up of the home is rebellion against the family, God's first institution. Another perversion of people is homosexuality. Satan uses all these things, and so much more, against God's creation because he hates God and hates those who are created in His image.

> *When you belong to Jesus, you are free.*

Satan believes people should be used as pawns in his battle against God. He deceives people into saying, "I don't want to be a Christian. I want to be free!" Well, you're not free when you're not a Christian! You're bound in sin and death when you're Satan's property, and he just moves you around like a piece of driftwood.

When you belong to Jesus, you are free. People who turn from Christ are turning to darkness. Notice that when Judas walked away from Christ, he killed himself (Acts 1:16-19). As long as he walked with Jesus, he was walking in the Light. But when he walked away from Christ, he walked into darkness and lost his way. That's when he walked right into Satan's clutches.

I remember one time when we had a "March for Jesus" in Denver, Colorado. People were protesting us and carrying signs that said, "Jesus is a myth. He was never here." I thought, that comes straight from Satan's heart. He always wants to say that Jesus is a myth and He doesn't love or care about you. Satan knows that for every person who accepts Christ as their Savior, he has lost another battle against God.

Even though he tricks people into believing his lies, Satan knows Jesus. The Word says that Jesus was with God from the very beginning (John 1:1); so, while Satan was still an angel in heaven, he knew Jesus. He believes strongly in the reality of who Jesus is and what He did on the Cross, that's why he tried to destroy Christ's work before it began by tempting Him in the wilderness (Luke 4:1-13).

Names of Satan

Just as God's names and titles reveal His loving and merciful nature, the names and titles of Satan describe his hideous character.

Satan's angelic name was Lucifer, which means "shining one."[1] But just as Abraham, Sarah, Israel, and Paul received new names when they entered into an eternal covenant with God, Lucifer's name was changed to indicate the "deal" he cut when he entered into rebellion. Immediately upon his fall, Lucifer's name was changed to Satan.

Satan in Hebrew means "an opponent, the archenemy of good, to attack, accuse, adversary." Satan is mankind's adversary (1 Peter 5:8). He is against you, and he does everything he can to make sure you stumble and fall.

Satan is the accuser of the brethren. He lurks in the shadows, watching your every move and, whenever you sin, he rushes to God's throne in heaven to accuse you:

> *And the LORD said unto Satan, From whence comest thou? And Satan answered the LORD, and said, From going to and fro in the earth, and from walking up and down in it. And the LORD said unto Satan, Hast thou considered my servant Job? ...And Satan answered the LORD, and said, Skin for skin, yea, all that a man hath will he give for his life. But put forth thine hand now, and touch his bone and his flesh, and he will curse thee to thy face.*
>
> Job 2:2-5

> *And the great dragon was cast out, that old serpent, called the devil, and Satan, which deceiveth the whole world: ....for the accuser of our brethren is cast down, which accused them before our God day and night.*
>
> Revelation 12:9,10

The good news is God doesn't listen to the devil! God says, "My child doesn't have any sin. He's as white as snow. He's washed in the blood of Jesus." Satan's accusations fall on deaf ears.

Satan is called the devil (Revelation 12:9). In Greek, *devil* is the word "diabolos," which means "a false accuser, slanderer."[2] And notice, if you take away the "d" in devil, what do you have? Evil! The devil is big-time evil. What is *evil*? It means "adversity, affliction, distress, grief, harm, mischief, sorrow, trouble, wretched, displease, vanity, unjust, slander, hurtful, vicious, and lewd." The devil is all these things and more!

Satan is also called the dragon: "...behold a great red dragon, having seven heads and ten horns, and seven crowns upon his heads" (Revelation 12:3). It's pretty easy to think of the devil as a dragon because the fairy tales children are told describe dragons as evil, with smoke flaring from their nostrils. A dragon always has to do with something destructive.

He is called the serpent (Genesis 3:1). When I think of a snake, I think of something sneaky that hides in the grass and slithers along real fast! He's very subtle and very beguiling because he doesn't want his prey to see him. Then he slips out and strikes his prey, paralyzing it with his venom or by strangling it to death, and then swallows it whole. This is what Satan does: he waits until a person is vulnerable and then he doesn't mess around—he devours his prey with one bite.

One of the major names of Satan is found in Ephesians 2:2: "...the prince of the power of the air...." A prince is someone who has an exalted position. Satan's authority is found in the atmosphere closest to the earth. He can move through the air at incredible speed, as fast as lightning (Luke 10:18).

Satan's authority over the powers of the air, however, is not going to last forever! When the Church is raptured before the Tribulation begins, Satan will do battle with the Archangel Michael and lose his abilities and authority over the powers of the air (Revelation 12:7-9).

Satan is also the prince of devils (Matthew 12:24), the prince of this world (John 12:31), profane wicked prince of Israel (Ezekiel 21:25), and chief prince of Meshech and Tubal (Ezekiel 38:2).

Jesus is the Prince. He's the Prince of Peace (Isaiah 9:6), the Prince of life (Acts 3:15), and the Prince of the kings of the earth (Revelation 1:5). That's why Satan gave himself the title of "prince"— he tries to magnify himself over God and Jesus. But the devil has authority over the air, devils, and people who refuse to give their hearts to God, whereas Jesus has authority over peace, life, and government!

Satan is also called the god of this world:

In whom the god of this world hath blinded the minds of them which believe not, lest the light of the glorious gospel of Christ, who is the image of God, should shine unto them.

2 Corinthians 4:4

Does this mean that Satan made the world? That he rules it? No! He is the god of pagan people. They worship him as Buddha, Krishna, a volcano, cow, tree, pop bottle, or piece of rock. He is their "god," and therefore he is called the god of this world.

Can you believe Satan is also called a king? He's the king of the bottomless pit. This kingdom is limited and is terribly disgusting: "...there arose a smoke out of the pit, as the smoke of the great furnace.... And there came out of the smoke locusts upon the earth..." (Revelation 9:2-3).

The pit is a smoky, intensely hot place where grotesque devils dwell. Satan is truly a sad, pitiful creature if he thinks that is something to be proud of.

More aspects of his dark character are shown in the other names Satan has as the king of the bottomless pit: "...in the Hebrew tongue [his name] is Abaddon, but in the Greek tongue hath his name Apollyon" (Revelation 9:11). The meaning of both Abaddon[3] and Apollyon[4] refers to "destroyer."

Satan is Beelzebub:

But when the Pharisees heard it, they said, This fellow doth not cast out devils, but by Beelzebub the prince of the devils.

Matthew 12:24

Beelzebub is Satan's most grotesque name. It means "god of flies."[5] He is the lord of the dunghill. He is the god of filth! Can you imagine somebody worshiping the lord of a dunghill? That's what you're doing when you sin—you are worshiping a garbage dump, and Satan will make you garbage too.

The devil is the tempter (Matthew 4:3). You must resist the devil because he is temptation itself. He will say to you, "You don't need to read your Bible today. You're spiritual enough. You don't need to pray every day." That's temptation and it comes straight from the devil's own mouth! Decide to whom you are going to listen to. If you listen to temptation, you are listening to your enemy who only wants to kill you. You can overcome temptation the same way you overcome the devil—you resist him and speak the Word (James 4:7; 1 Peter 5:8).

Satan is the one who gets people into pornography. He perverted sex! If you have ever heard demons scream out of somebody's mouth, they always use filthy language. You don't want Satan around because he'll make you filthy—in your thoughts, words, and actions. He'll have you doing things that you never would have thought of doing until you let him entertain your mind with his filth.

You cannot afford any part of his uncleanness in your life. If you have pornography in your possession, if you are watching "R"-rated movies (or worse), or if you are involved in anything that is unclean, then get rid of it! Get somebody to pray with you about these areas where the devil has gained a hold on you. This filthiness is dangerous.

Satan is the spirit of rebellion who claims your children and leads them on the path to destruction. He is the "...spirit that now worketh in children of disobedience" (Ephesians 2:2).

My husband Wally and I had a relative who was oppressed by a rebellious spirit most of his life. For 30 years he lived a rebellious, homosexual lifestyle. He told my husband and me that he was blinded by the devil. "I thought I was born a homosexual. That this was the way I had to be. But the Bible says that nobody is born a homosexual. I was blind to all that."

This man received Christ as his Savior, and because he was so Word-washed and turned on to the Lord, he helped others get free. "Behind all of those lies was the devil," he said. "It was the god of this world who wanted me to live that way." Thank God this man finally recognized and was delivered from that spirit of disobedience; he walked the Holy Ghost way until the day he died, and went to be with the Lord!

Personality Profile

Satan's personality is rotten. His emotions are putrid, his will is to take people down a dirty path, and his actions are always sinful.

> *If [satan] can get you discouraged and depressed, then he can snare you and suck the spiritual life out of you.*

Satan has emotions. Revelation 12:17 says the devil was "wroth," which means he was angry. I don't believe Satan has any good emotions, but he has plenty of negative ones.

He has a will: "And that they may recover themselves out of the snare of the devil, who are taken captive by him at his will" (2 Timothy 2:26). The devil wants to take everyone captive. That is his will for you. And he constantly tries to force his will on you. If he can get you discouraged and depressed, then he can snare you and suck the spiritual life out of you.

He is a confirmed sinner. First John 3:8 says "...for the devil sinneth from the beginning...." His nature became sin, and he wants the whole world to be like him.

Satan is sneaky and subtle. Second Corinthians 11:3 says that just as the devil subtly corrupted Eve into sinning, he will also try to corrupt your mind "...from the simplicity that is in Christ." Satan will try to deceive you into believing that God and salvation should be more complex.

In other words, he will lure you away from Christ by making you think you are too smart for God. He will make you say, "The Bible is filled with inaccuracies. Science has shown that the world couldn't have been made in six days. I couldn't receive salvation by just saying a simple prayer. I'm too smart to believe that."

When God talks to me, He speaks very simply. Why? Because the Holy Spirit gets right to the heart of the matter, so He can correct and direct me without confusing me or getting me off-track.

I like to think of God's directions as being much like road signs, which simply say, "Stop," "Yield," or "Exit 1 Mile." You understand these directions immediately. You know exactly what they mean because they leave little room for confusion or doubt.

Road signs are simple because people need to understand them. They don't say, "Because of the amount of traffic in this area and the high ratio of accidents for this particular intersection, the elected representatives of this city have made it a law that you must bring your vehicle to a complete stop and then proceed cautiously. Failure to abide by this law will result in a fine." No one would be able to read this sign. As a result, people would fail to stop, there would be accidents, and people would get hurt.

The devil would like for you to believe that God should speak to you in a high and lofty manner. If He did, you would never be able to understand what God said, would you? Salvation is easy for you to receive because God doesn't want anyone to miss out:

For God so loved the world, that he gave his only begotten Son, that whosoever believeth in him should not perish, but have everlasting life.

John 3:16

This message may be simple. Although it may not challenge you intellectually, it saves you completely! The devil is defeated with this simple phrase, and you are made victorious.

CHAPTER 2

Twisted Game Plan: Wiles of the Enemy

Satan hates you. He has despised and detested you from the very foundation of the world. From the moment he was kicked out of paradise and saw Adam and Eve strolling with God in the garden that used to be his, he has made it his work to destroy, terrify, and keep people from developing a relationship with God. In this chapter we're going to look at his game plan for achieving that objective.

Even though the devil wants you to believe that he has the power to destroy you, as a Christian you have full authority over him. You don't have to be afraid of him—he is afraid of you. Not only for your authority, but for the powerful spiritual weapons available to you to stop his attacks. For instance, when he comes to attack you, all you have to do is speak the Word and resist him, and he will have to flee (James 4:7; Revelation 12:11).

Expert at Deception

Remember, Satan is a thief, a murderer, and a destroyer; the main way he can accomplish all this is through deception. In fact, his very first act was to deceive Eve.

When Satan met Eve in the Garden of Eden, he did four things to deceive her. (See Genesis 3.) Firstly, he didn't appear as a beast, but as a creature she saw every day, a snake. Secondly, he questioned God's Word. Thirdly, he offered her something that sounded better than what she thought she had.

Lastly, he made God appear to be a liar. He said, "God told you not to eat from that tree because He doesn't want you to be as wise as He is. God lied when He said you would die if you ate from that tree. You won't really die." The devil told Eve that God's Word wasn't true. The devil said only he would tell her the truth.

Satan does the same thing to you. He says, "God doesn't want you to be healed. He doesn't want you to prosper. Those promises are meant for His 'pets': His Word only applies to the people He really loves." The devil doesn't tell you the truth. The Word says he is the father of lies (John 8:44); and he lies to you so he can steal from you, murder you, and devour you.

The devil appealed to Eve in three areas: 1) to eat something which was forbidden—the lust of the flesh; 2) he told her she would be wise the lust of the eyes; 3) and that she would be like God—the pride of life.

Satan used the same three lusts to tempt Jesus in the wilderness. Satan came against Jesus with the lust of the flesh:

And when he [Jesus] *had fasted forty days and forty nights, he was afterward an hungred. And when the tempter came to him, he said, If thou be the Son of God, command that these stones be made bread. But he answered and said, It is written, Man shall not live by bread alone, but by every word that proceedeth out of the mouth of God.*

Matthew 4:2-4

Satan used prestige and honor to tempt Him with the lusts of the eyes:

And the devil, taking him up into an high mountain, shewed unto him all the kingdoms of the world in a moment of time. And the devil said unto him, All this power will I give thee, and the glory of them: for that is delivered unto me; and to whomsoever I will I give it. If thou therefore wilt worship me, all shall be thine. And Jesus answered and said unto him, Get thee behind me, Satan: for it is written, Thou shalt worship the Lord thy God, and him only shalt thou serve.

Luke 4:5-8

Satan tempted Him with the pride of life:

Then the devil taketh him up into the holy city, and setteth him on a pinnacle of the temple, And saith unto him, If thou be the Son of God, cast thyself down: for it is written, He shall give his angels charge concerning thee: and in their hands they shall bear thee up, lest at any time thou dash thy foot against a stone. Jesus said unto him, It is written again, Thou shalt not tempt the Lord thy God.

Matthew 4:5-7

How did Jesus overcome those temptations? He spoke the Word! And when He did, not only did the devil depart from Him, but God's angels came to minister to Him (Matthew 4:10-11), and He was filled with the power of the Holy Spirit (Luke 4:14).

> *When the devil tries to deceive you into sinning against God, you must speak the Word.*

When the devil tries to deceive you into sinning against God, you must speak the Word. However, in order to speak the Word, you must first read and memorize it. Start getting into the Bible today! It will defend you and give you the power to attack Satan (Ephesians 6:17). You will see that after you come through a temptation and stand on the Word, you will come out of your troubles with a new power and new anointing of the Holy Spirit. You will see who Christ is in you.

When Satan comes to deceive you, he won't come in a red suit with two horns and a pitchfork saying, "Today, I am going to tempt you in the area of the flesh," or "I'm going to steer you off God's path by getting you into pride." No, the devil appears as an angel of light and offers you a "better, easier" life. He'll say, "I want you to have a good time. This religion bit is really crowding your style. You could be free, and you could make a lot of money, and you could have a lot of fun." He's very sneaky.

17

The devil tried to deceive Job by physically attacking him so he could gain possession of Job's mind. The devil killed Job's children, took his wealth, and stole his health. He made Job think that God did all this to him. His goal was to have Job denounce and curse God.

The devil will use your friends and loved ones to speak his lies. The devil didn't kill Job's wife because he could use her to torment and harass him (Job 2:9-10)! Then Job's three friends came along and gave him a hard time, asking him what he did wrong that would make God do this to him. They said, "This kind of crisis wouldn't have come if you hadn't blown it someplace."

Have you faced troubles and losses like Job did? Often, when people experience the death of a loved one, illness, or financial difficulties, they come to me and ask, "What did I do wrong? Why is God punishing me?" I say, "God didn't do this to you! The devil did. God is the One who will help you. Turn to God, and let Him minister His peace and love to you." It is so easy for people to be deceived by Satan when they face problems. That's why you need to stand on God's Word.

The devil will deceive you into quitting. Maybe you have a job that you don't like or an employer who harasses you and gives you a hard time. Satan will whisper, "Quit!" But will you listen to the devil, who always gives you the "easy" way out? No!

When you follow God's will for your life, it isn't always easy. Jesus said: "...strait is the gate, and narrow is the way, which leadeth unto life, and few there be that find it" (Matthew 7:14).

The devil doesn't want you going the narrow way because there you will find eternal life. He wants you to wander aimlessly—right into his pit.

The devil deceived Job into believing that his circumstances would never change and that Job should end it all. Job didn't "do" anything to deserve his situation, and there wasn't anything he could "do" to get out of it. The devil caused Job's grief; and only God could deliver him.

The devil told Job that because he was such a pillar of the community and a godly man that he deserved better in life. Satan lured Job into believing self-righteousness was more important than God's righteousness. The devil pointed to Job's works and said, "You don't deserve this." Job was not looking to God in faith.

Do you have a difficult marriage? A child who never seems to act sweet or listen to you? A physical condition that persists and torments you after long weeks and months and years of prayer? Those long-term situations are hard, and Satan knows it. That's why he brings strife into your life. But don't let these problems deceive you into "quitting." Instead, let them bring you closer to God, deeper in prayer, and further into the Word.

When Jesus left the wilderness after the devil tempted Him, He came out with a fresh anointing of the Holy Spirit (Luke 4:14). Likewise, when you go through a difficult situation by standing on the Word, you will be the victor. In your troubles, you will see who Christ is in you and who you are as a child of God. You will leave your wilderness with the power of the Holy Spirit, who will help and comfort you (John 15:26).

"Money Talks"

The devil is at work in the world's monetary and commercial systems. Satan has always been involved in money, because the Word says the root of all evil is the love of money (1 Timothy 6:10). The creator of evil was the devil. So, when you covet things, you put them on a pedestal and place them above God—that is the sin of idolatry.

Satan gets people to the place where they don't want anyone to take their money or things away from them, and they certainly don't want God to have any of it either. By this time they have become so greedy that they yield themselves more and more to the devil—they are his. First John 2:15 says:

Love not the world, neither the things that are in the world. If any man love the world, the love of the Father is not in him. For all that is in the world, the lust of the flesh, and the lust of the eyes, and the pride of life, is not of the Father, but is of the world.

The devil will use the glitter and glamour of the world to entice you and use your cravings to trap you into wanting even more. Have you noticed that the more you crave and the more you get, the less happy you are? Proverbs 27:20 says:

Hell and destruction are never full; so the eyes of man are never satisfied.

Things won't bring you happiness, only God's love can make you happy. Your spirit knows this, but your greed has blocked the paths of communication from your spirit to your mind.

Have you heard the saying, "Money talks"? Well, guess who makes money talk? The devil. He knows that by controlling the world's monetary systems, he will control the entire world. He knows that if he can tempt you through money, he can get a hold of you in other areas as well. If he can get you into money, he can get you away from God. Jesus said, you cannot love God and money (Matthew 6:24 NIV). Why? Because God has power and money has power, and the two cannot work together.

But they that will be rich fall into temptation and a snare, and into many foolish and hurtful lusts, which drown men in destruction and perdition. For the love of money is the root of all evil: which while some coveted after, they have erred from the faith, and pierced themselves through with many sorrows.

1 Timothy 6:9,10

Many people who fall in love with money cheat their families. They ignore their children. They lie. Their reputations go down the drain because of the underhanded things they do. Their homes break up. They steal. I have even heard of people who died of starvation when they had $100,000 stashed away in tin cans buried in the backyard. None of these actions are from God. These kind of actions are fueled by the devil.

Go to now, ye rich men, weep and howl for your miseries that shall come upon you. Your riches are corrupted, and your garments are moth eaten. Your gold and silver is cankered; and the rust of them shall be a witness against you and shall eat your flesh as it were fire. Ye have heaped treasure together for the last days. Behold, the hire of the labourers who have reaped down your fields, which is of you kept back by fraud, crieth: and the cries of them which have reaped are entered into the ears of the Lord of Sabaoth. Ye have lived in pleasure on the earth, and been wanton; ye have nourished your hearts, as in a day of slaughter. Ye have condemned and killed the just; and he doth not resist you.

James 5:1-6

I didn't always believe that money corrupted people. However, after more than 40 years of working in the ministry, I have seen the devil use God's gift of prosperity against people. I've seen people at our church, Orchard Road Christian Center, begin to prosper. They lovingly give their tithes to God, but pretty soon they begin to look at their money more than they look to God. The devil gives them cravings for more money and more things, and they start to follow after "stuff" instead of God. Their love of money drives them from the faith and pierces their hearts with acute mental and emotional pain.

For Ananias and Sapphira, the love of money cost them their lives. They gave in to greed, and they lied to the Holy Spirit about how much money they had profited from the sale of their land. Both died on the spot (see Acts 5).

Political Arena

The devil is at work against national leaders. Daniel 10:13 gives evidence of this when an angel tells Daniel of a fallen angel (the prince of the kingdom of Persia) who was struggling against God's angel: "But the prince of the kingdom of Persia withstood me [God's angel] one and twenty days: but, lo, Michael, one of the chief princes, came to help me; and I remained there with the kings of Persia."

Daniel saw Satan's evil angels controlling nations, but he also saw the power that is unleashed when God's people pray and get into spiritual warfare—the powers of darkness over nations can be broken.

The devil wants kings and leaders of nations because he wants power. The devil thinks that if he gets the heart of a king, he will get the entire nation. But the Bible says, "The king's heart is in the hand of the LORD, as the rivers of water: he turneth it whithersoever he will." I believe every Christian should pray for one nation and leader every day:

*I exhort therefore, that, ...prayers, intercessions, ...be made for all men;
For kings, and for all that are in authority; that we may lead a quiet and
peaceable life in all godliness and honesty.*

1 Timothy 2:1,2

If you don't pray for the leaders of nations, the devil may get them! Pray honest men and women into power, and pray peace for all people.

God can take the heart of a king and turn it the way He wills; but He does this only through prayer. This is shown in the book of Daniel when Nebuchadnezzar's heart was turned totally toward God. Then, when Daniel ministered to Cyrus, the king of Persia, God took Cyrus's heart in His hand and turned it the way He wanted it to go. Still later, God took the heart of another Persian king, Darius, and had him help the Israelites rebuild the Temple. None of these men would have changed their hearts if someone—Daniel or the entire nation of Israel—had not prayed for them.

You, too, need to pray for nations and leaders. When you watch the news, don't just feel sad about it and say, "The devil is at it again." Say, "Devil, in the name of Jesus, I command you to leave that place and to leave those people alone. God, I ask you to heal that nation and to move on the hearts of its leaders to bring peace and security to these people." Take authority over Satan. If you don't move in on it, the devil will.

Crime and Violence

The devil is involved in crime. He was the one who created it, and every day his work bears a little more fruit. Since the early 1980s, gangs have become more and more prevalent. If you pray against these gangs, things will change. For instance, I had prayed for years against the Mafia in America and that it would be brought to confusion. I didn't see any fruit until recently, when I read a news article that said the American Mafia system had fallen apart and was just not making it because too many mafiosos were getting saved!

If you prayed as much as you talked about crime in America, you would see something happen in gangs and other problems going on in the streets. A woman in our church witnessed to a co-worker about the power of prayer over crime, and she was rewarded with this powerful testimony:

A co-worker's son was being pressured by peers and gang members to join the gangs. Many of his friends had joined the gangs, but he resisted. After he graduated from high school, gang members still threatened, harassed, and tried to intimidate him into joining, but he continued to resist. I prayed for my co-worker and witnessed to her, telling her to speak the Word over her children.

I told my co-worker to apply the blood of Jesus over her son and her family (by speaking that they were covered in Jesus' blood), *speak the Word, and place a blood line around her home* (again, by speaking it).

During Christmas break, my co-worker told me that she had a dream and had seen her son lying dead in a coffin. She woke up immediately, knelt beside her bed, and began to pray. She prayed to God to save her son and turn whatever was meant for evil around for good. She began to apply the blood of Jesus over him.

Whenever she thought about the dream for the next week, she prayed and applied the blood of Jesus over her son and his family (wife and two young children). *Then, several days before Christmas, her son and his family were at home when someone knocked at their door. When her son asked who it was, the people lied and said it was a friend. When he opened the door, three gang members came in with their guns drawn.*

One of them pushed her son down on the couch in the front room and put a gun to the back of his head. The gang member cocked his gun, but he couldn't shoot him. He told her son several times that he was going to kill him. The other gang members took the wife and children into another room and began to shoot their guns. My co-worker's son jumped up and ran into the other room, thinking they had shot his family, but they had shot up the ceiling.

The gang member brought him back into the living room, pushed him down to the floor, placed the gun to the front of his head, and cocked the gun. But he still could not shoot him. Instead, the gang members robbed the family of all their Christmas money and left.

My co-worker's son recognized one of the gang members and ran to the door and called out his name. The three gang members turned and began to shoot up the apartment. They shot up the door, windows, walls, and ceiling. Bullets were flying everywhere, but neither he nor his wife and children were shot. My co-worker said she knew that because she prayed and applied the blood that God saved her son's life and family. The police have since arrested the three gang members, and they are all in jail.

My co-worker prays, reads the Bible, and pleads the blood over her family daily. She says her son does not hang around gang members and keeps away from these friends. She prays to God that when someone tries to hurt her son, they would not be able to and they wouldn't know why. She learned that the prayer, the Word, and the blood of Jesus do work!

Being a Christian doesn't mean you're just a flicker of light on the earth; you are a declaration of the power of God! So when you see that the devil has overtaken an area with crime, bind that stronghold and tell the devil to pack his bags and get out!

False Religions

The devil has laid the foundations, from the time of the Tower of Babel (see Genesis 11), for all types of false religions. He has given these religions "supreme beings," doctrines, and "steps" to get to heaven. People yearning for spiritual fulfillment flock to these religions, hoping desperately that their deeds will set their spirits free. Instead, they have put their spirits into eternal bondage because they chose to believe a lie instead of the truth.

Sickness and Disease

Health care has never been more readily available nor more advanced than in the beginning half of the twenty-first century. Yet, more people are falling apart than ever before.

My grandparents died of tuberculosis when they were very young—my grandmother was 27 and my grandfather was 34. When a cure was found, tuberculosis remained a serious disease, but with treatment it wasn't deadly. But now, tuberculosis is back as a fatal illness. Can you imagine, here we are in this enlightened day and people are dying from things that we thought we cured 50 years ago.

What's behind all this disease? The devil! God doesn't send sickness, He sent the cure—Jesus Christ. Satan has been busy pouring out plagues upon mankind throughout time; but new and increasingly bizarre illnesses have been arising in these end times.

> *God doesn't send sickness, He sent the cure—Jesus Christ.*

We see the devil working in the area of illness in the Bible. Satan smote Job with body sores from the soles of his feet to the crown of his head. When his friends came to comfort him, they barely recognized him! Who put this sickness on Job? Satan. Who healed him? God.

The devil afflicts people with handicaps, making them (among other things) deaf and mute:

> *As they went out, behold, they brought to him a dumb man possessed with a devil. And when the devil was cast out, the dumb spake....*
>
> Matthew 9:32,33

Now, not all handicaps come from demons, but the devil is the one who causes the afflictions. (See Matthew 12:22; Luke 13:11-13.)

The devil makes people insane; and he doesn't afflict only adults, he especially likes to afflict children because in doing so, he also torments the parents:

> *Lord, have mercy on my son: for he is lunatick, and sore vexed: for ofttimes he falleth into the fire, and oft into the water. And Jesus rebuked the devil; and he departed out of him: and the child was cured from that very hour.*
>
> Matthew 17:15,18

How this father must have suffered! It was a tragic situation. He had to watch over his child all the time or the boy would burn or drown himself. The father couldn't take his eyes off his child for one minute because the devil had a stranglehold on him. The disciples couldn't help him; only Jesus Himself could release the boy from the devil's grip (Matthew 17:16-18).

Do you think God would want His people not to think clearly? Not at all. God gave His people the mind of Christ (1 Corinthians 2:16)! It is Satan who tries to steal your clarity of thought from you, because without it, you cannot have a true relationship with God.

General sicknesses, such as colds and flu, are from the devil. He weakens people with the flu and keeps them from church with a cold. Not everyone who gets sick is oppressed by a demon, but they are being attacked by the devil.

The devil will hit you with every bacteria and virus under the sun because he knows if he can get a stronghold of infirmity in your body, he can wipe you out. You have to resist the enemy. You have to ask for people to lay hands on you and speak the Word over your body. Ask Jesus Christ for His healing touch, because He is the One who will heal you.

Even when you have the sniffles, look to Jesus to heal you. He cures every disease, infirmity, and weakness: "And Jesus went about all Galilee...healing all manner of sickness and all manner of disease among the people" (Matthew 4:23).

Perverting Moral Attitudes

The devil has been the busiest of all in this area since the 1960s. Many people today don't have morals; they believe in doing what they feel like doing. Satan has done everything he can to eliminate standards of conduct.

When I was in public school, we prayed in the morning, said the Pledge of Allegiance to the Flag, and learned the Ten Commandments. Learning those guidelines for living was helpful to us and was a blessing. We knew how to treat people, and, in turn, we were treated well.

The devil doesn't want you to know how to act; he wants you to react in selfishness because when you react this way, you are protecting yourself. You don't think about what the other person is feeling, so you do the things that will further your ambitions and do the most for you.

Immorality is rampant in the whole world, and the consequences have been chaos and death. God set up a system of morality for you to follow so you could be healthy and happy and protect others from pain. The devil has perverted people's attitudes towards morality, making them believe that God created morals to restrain them and keep them in line. People nowadays think it is such a joke to be immoral—but they are laughing their way to hell.

Sowing Tares Among the Wheat

The devil is hard at work in the Christian Church, trying to divide it so it will fall. He loves to divide Christians: he likes to divide Christian mates, Christian parents and children, Christian friends, Christian prayer partners, and Christian churches. That's one of his major weapons.

He tempts Christians to lie. When you accuse and slander a Christian, you become like the devil, who accuses and slanders Christians to the Father: "...for the accuser of our brethren is cast down, which accused them before our God day and night" (Revelation 12:10).

Satan employs devils and demons against Christians. Sometimes, when I get up in the morning, I can feel the different types of demons he has sent against me for that day. He tries to throw monkey wrenches into every work a person does for God, and he knows which specific demon—whether it be a spirit of lust, pride, anger, or slander—to send to defeat a specific project. When this happens, I do what the Word says and put on the whole armor of God to do battle against these demonic powers (Ephesians 6:11-17).

The devil sows tares among the believers. He comes to church; and I believe there are unsaved people who come to church to cause problems in the name of the devil. They are sent by Satan. They act religious, but they do not have anything in their hearts for God.

The devil incites persecution against Christians. He would like to kill you; but you have a defense—Jesus, your Intercessor. You need to get bold against the devil and keep coming against him, pleading the blood of Jesus over yourself and your situation.

The only way you're going to break the devil's power in any of these areas is through intensive prayer and the Word. When you get as stubborn with him as he is with you, you will win because you have God's Word, Jesus' name, His blood, and an avenue of prayer. And remember, God is all-powerful, Jesus is seated at His right hand, and all the angels and authorities are at your bidding.

So, can you break Satan's power over these bad situations? Absolutely! I will talk more about this in the next chapter.

CHAPTER 3

Forces of Darkness: Structure, Rank, and Responsibility

The whole world lieth in wickedness.

1 John 5:19

Evil spirits are roaming the earth more now than ever before. There is more occult, more strife, more confusion, more unclean spirits all over the world. Why? Because Satan knows his time is short, and he has released many of his devils and demons so he can rip this world and its people apart in the little time he has left.

Satan is preparing the world for the Antichrist. If the Antichrist had been introduced 20 years ago, people wouldn't have been ready. People would have said, "We don't want this man, there is something wrong with him." The more evil spirits oppress and possess people and cause them to deny the Bible and the reality of Christ, to murder people, and to get into sexual perversion, the more people become willing to accept an absolutely evil leader.

Jesus told us in the parable of the wheat and the tares that an increase in the number of evil people would happen in the end times. He said a farmer planted good wheat seeds, but his enemy secretly planted tares (weeds) in the field. When the servants wanted to pull the weeds, the farmer told them to leave the weeds alone, "...lest while ye gather up the tares, ye root up also the wheat with them. Let both grow together until the harvest: and in the time of harvest I will say to the reapers, Gather ye together first the tares, and bind them in bundles to burn them: but gather the wheat into my barn" (Matthew 13:29-30).

Jesus was saying, leave the evil people alone because some of them could be born again. If these people were plucked from the earth too soon, they wouldn't be given the full opportunity to make a decision for Christ. "Wait till the end of this age," He said, "because then we will know which people truly belong to God, and which have sold themselves out to the devil."

The meaning of the bizarre and violent occurrences in today's world can be explained only by understanding the powers behind them. The conflicts we see are not battles of flesh and blood, but a spiritual war that Satan and his army are waging against God and His army.

God's army is headed by God the Father, Jesus, and the Holy Ghost. Below them in rank are angels and Christians. Likewise, Satan's army has a hierarchy and structure, and because Satan is neither all-knowing nor all-powerful, he has to delegate responsibilities and be very organized.

The evil army is made up of Satan, his fallen angels, demons, and unbelievers. Satan is the "commander in chief ." Beneath him are the fallen angels, whom we call "devils." They are in charge of the demons, which we know as evil or unclean spirits. The final layer of this evil organization is made up of humans who knowingly or unknowingly give their allegiance to Satan.

Each devil and demon is given a rank and responsibility within this army. This structure is spelled out in Ephesians 6:12: "For we wrestle not against flesh and blood, but against principalities, against powers, against the rulers of the darkness of this world, against spiritual wickedness in high places."

The "privates" in Satan's army are the *principalities*, which are common demons that come against ordinary people, especially Christians, to attack, harass, and torment them.

The *powers* are the demons who have even greater authority and power. They oppress and possess some people who are in positions of leadership—people who control churches, businesses, schools, among other things.

Holding an even higher place of authority are *the rulers of darkness*, fallen angels who are assigned to oppress and attack cities.

The *spiritual wickedness in high places* are devils who are the "generals" in Satan's army. They steer national leaders and countries toward evil and are in command of the demons that oppress and possess some national leaders.

God is for you and has given you complete authority over these forces of darkness.

Are you thinking, *Wow, if all this is against me, how in the world do I stand a chance?* Not only do you "stand a chance," but you are guaranteed victory over this army. Always remember that "…If God be for us, who can be against us?" (Romans 8:31).

God is *for* you and has given you complete authority over these forces of darkness (Luke 10:19). You can overcome these dominions at any level (whether it be powers, principalities, rulers of darkness, or spiritual wickedness) with the three weapons in your arsenal—God's Word, prayer, and fasting.

Daniel used these three weapons for 21 days to overcome the prince of the kingdom of Persia. This prince was a devil that was controlling Cyrus, the king of Persia. This devil was stronger than God's angel, but when Daniel spoke the Word, prayed, and fasted for three weeks, the archangel Michael came to do battle with this devil and won (see Daniel 10).

Your prayers can put a thousand demons to flight. When you join your prayers with another believer, you put ten thousand demons to flight (Deuteronomy 32:30). When you speak God's Word, heaven moves to do your bidding (Matthew 18:18). So, when you pray God's Word and couple that with fasting, you are putting the forces of heaven at war against the forces of hell, and you know that God always wins.

Fallen Angels

Devils are the angels that chose to follow Lucifer in rebellion. These angels had helped Lucifer cover God's throne and helped protect God's holiness; but they followed Satan in his rebellion and fell with him. They were swept down to earth and became Satan's generals (Revelation 12:4). They have the same goal as their evil "commander in chief," and that is to torment, harass, and hurt people.

Jesus spoke of "the devil and his angels" (Matthew 25:41), and John spoke of "the dragon ...and his angels" (Revelation 12:7). They are intelligent beings that are under the leadership of Satan, have superhuman intelligence and superphysical strength, and are contending for mastery over the bodies and minds of all members of the human race.

Revelation 12:4 speaks of the dragon sweeping a third of the stars of heaven down with his tail. *Stars* in this verse is a picture of angels. Satan caused a third of the heavenly host to rebel with him when he tried to be like God. Since all God's angels are without number " ...ten thousand times ten thousand, and thousands of thousands" (Revelation 5:11), the number of Satan's angels is also tremendous.

Devils have doctrines: "Now the Spirit speaketh expressly, that in the latter times some shall depart from the faith, giving heed to seducing spirits, and doctrines of devils" (1 Timothy 4:1).

God's Word gives us pictures of these devils, and they are grotesque. John shows us the devils that will be loosed from the bottomless pit during the Tribulation:

> *And the shapes of the locusts were like unto horses prepared unto battle; and on their heads were as it were crowns like gold, and their faces were as the faces of men. And they had hair as the hair of women, and their teeth were as the teeth of lions. And they had breastplates, as it were breastplates of iron; and the sound of their wings was as the sound of chariots of many horses running to battle. And they had tails like unto scorpions, and there were stings in their tails....*
>
> Revelation 9:7-10

These devils were the angels Jude spoke about: "And the angels which kept not their first estate, but left their own habitation, he hath reserved in everlasting chains under darkness unto the judgment of the great day" (Jude 1:6).

I believe these angels were put into the chains of the bottomless pit because they were the "sons of God" who cohabited with women in Genesis 6:2-4 and created a race of giants.

Earthly Origin

Although devils have their origin in heaven, demons' origins are earth—the pre-Adamic earth.

> *In the beginning God created the heaven and the earth. And the earth was without form, and void; and darkness was upon the face of the deep....*
>
> Genesis 1:1,2

God created heaven and earth perfectly. He didn't do it halfway—it was a perfect, glorious creation. However, something very serious happened between the first and second verses of Genesis 1 because God's perfect creation was transformed into something that was without form.

I believe what happened was Satan's doing. After he fell from heaven to earth, he destroyed what God had created, and part of that creation was a race of people (Jeremiah 4:23-26; 2 Peter 3:5-6). Satan destroyed these people by leading them astray, and when they followed him, God brought judgment on the earth.

During the days of Noah, God also wanted to bring judgment on the earth and destroy it:

> *And God saw that the wickedness of man was great in the earth, and that every imagination of the thoughts of his heart was only evil continually. And it repented the LORD that he had made man on the earth, and it grieved him at his heart. And the LORD said, I will destroy man whom I have created from the face of the earth; both man, and beast, and the creeping thing, and the fowls of the air; for it repenteth me that I have made them. But Noah found grace in the eyes of the LORD.*
>
> Genesis 6:5-8

Notice God wanted to destroy the world, but the presence of one holy man made Him change His mind.

When the pre-Adamic race of people followed Satan and became evil, God decided to destroy the world. I believe He looked for one righteous person, but couldn't find one holy person in the bunch! So God destroyed the world, and these unredeemed, evil people were killed.

When the earth ended up in chaos (when it was without form and void), the spirits of these people came under Satan's domain. Their spirits remained on earth and, when God repopulated the earth, they set about to find a human being to enter into so they could express themselves.

These demons are known as jealous spirits, familiar spirits, deceiving spirits, and spirits of strife, confusion, and division. Their job is to get ahold of people and keep them from going to church, to get people to reject and wander away from the Christian faith, and to deceive people into believing that the true spiritual authorities are witches and psychics, not preachers of God's Word.

Jesus speaks about demon spirits in Matthew 12:43-45:

When the unclean spirit is gone out of a man, he walketh through dry places, seeking rest, and findeth none. Then he saith, I will return into my house from whence I came out; and when he is come, he findeth it empty, swept, and garnished. Then goeth he, and taketh with himself seven other spirits more wicked than himself, and they enter in and dwell there: and the last state of that man is worse than the first....

Devils don't come into human beings because they have their own form of expression as angels. Demons, however, only have expression when they are using a person. This is called demonic oppression or possession, depending on whether or not demons have invaded the body and soul (oppression) or the spirit (possession).

Although demons can possess only non-Christians, they can oppress anyone. Demons have specific targets—they oppress and possess people who are in leadership because these people have power, and Satan has always tried to get more and more power. Through these leaders Satan has the power to control a whole church, business organization, or country, and can turn them toward evil.

Jezebel was demon possessed. She was the high priestess of Baal, the god of the Canaanites, and she led the nation of Israel into the worship of this disgusting idol. Eventually, the people of Israel paid a terrible price for their idolatry. They were taken from their homeland and driven to a foreign land. I believe some of the leaders we see today who are murdering their own people are demon possessed.

When someone who is possessed of a demon dies, that spirit immediately seeks a dwelling place in another person (Matthew 12:43-45). It cannot walk into just any person's life; it must find one with an open door. If it is a spirit of lust, it seeks a lustful person. If it is a spirit of anger, it seeks to possess a person who has little control over his temper. A spirit of insanity will seek to enter a person's mind.

Personality Profile

Demons are lustful and adulterous spirits that seduce and deceive people, getting them into sin. These are powerful spirits, and I believe they have a tight grip on most of America.

When people get into lust and sexual perversion, they are committing a sin of the flesh. Although it isn't demon oppression at first, the sinful acts open the door for demons to influence fleshly desires: "Now the works of the flesh are manifest, which are these; Adultery, fornication, uncleanness, laciviousness, idolatry, witchcraft, hatred, variance, emulations, wrath, strife, seditions, heresies, envyings, murders, drunkenness, revellings, and such like..." (Galatians 5:19-21).

Once this happens, the person becomes oppressed with the spirits of lust and adultery. Demons then have control and get the person into a lifestyle that can go from perverse to downright satanic. These people can't stop themselves. They can't stop sinning. (See 2 Peter 2:14.)

Demons are ugly and can physically dwell inside the body of a person:

And I saw three unclean spirits like frogs come out of the mouth of the dragon, and out of the mouth of the beast, and out of the mouth of the false prophet.

Revelation 16:13

Demons vary in power: "...This kind can come forth by nothing, but by prayer and fasting" (Mark 9:29). Matthew 8:29 says they know the names of those who rebuke them and cast them out. In Acts 19:15, an evil spirit said, "...Jesus I know, and Paul I know; but who are ye?"

Demons believe in God and "tremble" (James 2:19). Their belief, however, is not one of faith, trust, and commitment; it is one of knowledge.

Demons also have willpower: "When the unclean spirit is gone out of a man, ...he saith, I will return into my house from whence I came out..." (Matthew 12:43-44).

They oppose Christians, trying to keep them from Satan's army: "Devils and Demons knowing God and His love: For I am persuaded, that neither .. . angel, nor principalities, nor powers...shall be able to separate us from the love of God, which is in Christ Jesus our Lord" (Romans 8:38-39).

Although these demons and devils have destructive abilities, the most important thing you can remember is Jesus has the ultimate authority over devils, demons, and Satan himself. When Jesus went to sit at the right hand of the Father in heaven, "...angels and authorities and powers [were] made subject unto him" (1 Peter 3:22). When you tell them to stop in Jesus' name, they must stop!

The Bible also speaks of "familiar spirits." These evil spirits operate in many ways. Among other things, they claim to know the future, impersonate the dead, and start and perpetuate family curses. (For information on family curses, read my book, *Break the Generation Curse*, which can be ordered from this ministry.)

An example of this is when Saul sought the counsel of the Witch of Endor: "Then said Saul unto his servants, Seek me a woman that hath a familiar spirit, that I may go to her, and enquire of her.... Then said the woman, Whom shall I bring up unto thee? And he said, Bring me up Samuel. And when the woman saw Samuel, she cried with a loud voice..." (1 Samuel 28:7,11-12).

A presence was in their midst and looked and talked like Samuel. The spirit even spoke the truth—up to a point. He knew Saul's sins and how God was going to punish him, but he didn't get everything exactly right. He said Saul would die the next day, but Saul died three days later (see 1 Samuel 31).

Demons have the power to do "lying signs and wonders." Take, for instance, the magicians at Pharaoh's court during Moses' time. These men turned their rods into serpents. Using demonic powers, they even duplicated several of the miracles Moses performed (see Exodus 7:10-12,19-22).

Both demons and devils are aware of two things—that Jesus is the Son of God and hell was created as their place of eternal torment. The devil and his army knows what the future holds for them, and they are trying to take as many people with them as possible!

Enemy Forces

In the United States Armed Forces, civilians do many of the jobs that soldiers don't have the time to do. Many times these people do janitorial, cashier, accounting, cooking, and other "hands-on" jobs on military bases around the world. These people are commanded by military personnel, but they are not considered soldiers.

The devil also uses "civilians" to do some of the work in his army. These humans knowingly or unknowingly give their allegiance to Satan and help him do his work. Anyone who sins and does not follow God's Word is serving Satan. As a Christian, you can serve Satan unknowingly and do his work if you don't know what God's Word says.

In his plan to torment and harass you, the devil will use strangers, loved ones, Christians, preachers *...anyone* who will listen to him. That's why you must put your confidence in the Lord, and not in people. Even Jesus didn't have a single person on whom He could rely. Judas betrayed him. Peter denied him. Peter, James, and John fell asleep when He needed them. Then, when He was in court, they all forsook him. If the devil used Jesus' disciples against Him, don't you think he'll use other Christians to attack you?

False Prophets

> *But there were false prophets also among the people, even as there shall be false teachers among you, who privily shall bring in damnable heresies, even denying the Lord....*
>
> 2 Peter 2:1

False prophets are part of the devil's army. They may claim to be Christians and to hear from God. They will say, "I have a word from the Lord for you. You're so spiritual, so deep. Other people don't understand this, but God's hands are upon you in such a wonderful way that you will understand."

These prophets will try to get you into pride, because once you love yourself more than you love the Lord, then the message you send to others will not be from God but from the devil.

Remember, no person is greater than anyone else. Only Jesus is the Great One! We are not to exalt ourselves or each other. We are only to exalt Jesus. The highest title any of us have on this earth is "servant." That's the title Jesus took.

When people begin to flatter you, exalt you, and give you little personal prophecies, you'd better watch out! When someone wants to prophesy anything to me, I say, "You have a word for me? Good. Let's go to my pastor and check it out because in the mouth of two or three witnesses everything is established." (See Matthew 18:16.)

Sometimes it's very hard to tell if a person is a false prophet because they will speak the Word and sometimes their prophecies are in line with what God has said. They seem so spiritual, but they are like their father, the devil, who is a liar (John 8:44).

The devil always lies, so even though a prophecy from an evil spirit can be mostly truth, there will be something that goes against God's Word. If any part of a prophecy goes against God's Word, then it is demon-inspired.

Eventually the false prophet will slip and say something out of line. That's why you need to pray against these false prophets because the demon spirits influencing them will try to keep the lost from hearing God's truth and steer Christians away from it.

When Paul was preaching the gospel in Philippi, a woman with the spirit of divination followed him and spoke a very religious-sounding message:

And it came to pass, as we went to prayer, a certain damsel possessed with a spirit of divination met us, which brought her masters much gain by soothsaying: The same followed Paul and us, and cried, saying, These men are the servants of the most high God, which shew unto us the way of salvation.

Acts 16:16,17

Through this woman, an evil spirit was saying all the right things. But after she did this for several days, Paul felt grieved in his spirit. The Holy Spirit showed him that something was wrong with the girl: "Paul...said to the spirit, I command thee in the name of Jesus Christ to come out of her. And he came out the same hour" (Acts 16:18).

Notice that Paul spoke to the spirit, not to the girl. Paul was not against the woman; he was against the spirit that possessed her body. Would you have been able to recognize this woman was possessed by an evil spirit? She was saying all the right things. She knew the spiritual status of these men. So wouldn't the spirit inside her be of God since she recognized these men preached salvation? No. Demons know enough of the Word to speak it in order to confuse you.

False Teachers

Demons oppress people who teach heresy (and, if these people are not Christians, they are probably possessed with demons). The false teachers use Scriptures to teach things that are not true. They teach that God is love; therefore, He wouldn't have sent His Son to die because that is not a loving thing to do. They teach that God's mercy would not allow someone to be condemned to hell, so the sacrifice of Christ was pointless.

39

The people who preach these things are false teachers. They teach you to follow things that are not godly, to do things that are not scriptural, and to come against the Church.

I've seen many people follow false teachers. They wander off and get into flaky stuff, even after my husband and I warned them that what they were getting into was not of God. It breaks my heart because when people become rebellious against God and don't serve Him, they start having problems. They die prematurely, their children are troubled, their marriages are broken, and so many other problems occur.

You must use spiritual discernment every time someone stands before you as a teacher. The devil loves to use false teachers because people usually believe what they hear from a pulpit or are taught in a Sunday school class. False teachers show you how to follow ungodly and unscriptural things.

False teachers prey on baby Christians and mature Christians who are eager to learn about God, and they fill them full of lies. They either take Scriptures out of context or they teach something without once turning to the Bible.

Know your Bible, read it, and pray that you comprehend it. Second Timothy 2:15 says: "Study to shew thyself approved unto God, a workman that needeth not to be ashamed, rightly dividing the word of truth." Otherwise, these people will lure you into false beliefs. Although you should appreciate and pray for preachers, you should always make sure their teaching is on solid, biblical ground.

Jesus recognized this problem during His day. He said to the Pharisees: "Ye are of your father the devil, ..." (John 8:44). The Pharisees were religious leaders who solidly upheld God's law. They knew the Word inside and out. They debated the meanings of Scriptures. They observed the holidays. They went to the Temple. But they were not God's men. They were the devil's.

False Tactics

False prophets and teachers exploit you because of greed. They don't care about you; they care about how much money you're going to give them:

"...through covetousness shall they with feigned words make merchandise of you..." (2 Peter 2:3).

I don't believe these people are deceived about their spiritual status. They do not believe they are Christians; they knowingly lead people off God's course. They are in the ministry because they want your money and your adoration. They don't care about you. They seem so spiritual, but they are deceptive. They stand in front of a choir, carry a Bible, and can even build your faith, but they are not sent from God.

False leaders are rebellious against any form of leadership. They think they know more than anybody else, even God: "But chiefly them that walk after the flesh in the lust of uncleanness, and despise government. Presumptuous are they, selfwilled, they are not afraid to speak evil of dignities" (2 Peter 2:10).

False teachers and prophets are riotous and live a double lifestyle: "And shall receive the reward of unrighteousness, as they that count it pleasure to riot in the day time. Spots they are and blemishes, sporting themselves with their own deceivings while they feast with you" (2 Peter 2:13).

A hair stylist at the shop where I get my hair done had been witnessing to the women he works with for quite a while. One day when I was in the shop, one of the women came to him in tears. She said that a friend had taken her to a church that Sunday and afterwards some of the young people took her to a bar to watch television.

Once they got her into the bar, they got her to drink. Then two of the men from the church tried to seduce her. She said, "I went to church to hear about God, but these people were trying to seduce me!" They were riotous. Thank God she had someone at work who witnesses the truth to her, because these people from the church were false teachers and were trying to lead her into sin.

These false teachers and prophets look for people like this girl who are not stable in their faith:

Having eyes full of adultery, and that cannot cease from sin; beguiling unstable souls: an heart they have exercised with covetous practices....

2 Peter 2:14

41

Stable people will quote God's Word; it is hard for them to be sucked into lies or false teachings. Stable people pray and can discern spirits. Unstable people believe anything they are told and follow any leader. That's why you need to get into the Word and follow it uncompromisingly!

Check It Out

The devil will sometimes use Christians to speak his lies. An example of this is when Jesus told the disciples that He was going to suffer and die. Peter said, "No, you're not!" Jesus said to Peter, "...Get thee behind me, Satan...." (Matthew 16:23). Psalm 22 and Matthew 16:21 said Jesus was going to suffer and die; so when Peter denied that He would be murdered, Jesus rebuked him because the words he spoke were not from God, but from the devil.

When you develop an intimate relationship with God and His Word, His voice becomes crystal clear to you.

Did Peter mean to speak against God's Word? No. He honestly believed that Christ would be protected from suffering and death. The devil likes to use this lie on us, too. Some people believe that because we are Christians we should be sheltered from pain. Jesus not only told us we would suffer, but we should expect to do so: "The servant is not greater than his lord. If they have persecuted me, they will also persecute you...." (John 15:20).

Peter's misguided statement didn't mean he was demon oppressed any more than our own belief in the devil's lies makes us sinful or demon oppressed. Peter was a solid Christian who loved the Lord very much. In fact, only minutes before Jesus rebuked him for what he said, Jesus had told Peter that he was the rock upon which the Church would be built (Matthew 16:17-19).

Even people who have the most intimate relationship with the Lord, who have laid a solid foundation for their lives on the Word, can be off-base and influenced by the devil. That's why you must always check out the prophecies that are spoken to you whether they be from a stranger, your pastor, or someone you hold in high esteem.

God will bring you to a place of peace and rest so that you can hear His still, small voice (1 Kings 19:12; Psalm 23:2). When you develop an intimate relationship with God and His Word, His voice becomes crystal clear to you: "And when he putteth forth his own sheep, he goeth before them, and the sheep follow him: for they know his voice. And a stranger will they not follow, but will flee from him: for they know not the voice of strangers" (John 10:4-5).

When you feel that you are allowing the noise of the world to crowd out God's leading, then pray this Scripture from John. When you give place to the Word instead of the world, your gentle Shepherd can lead you to safety and rest (Psalm 23:6).

Let's continue looking at spiritual warfare and very practical steps to Satan-proofing your life.

CHAPTER 4

———•◦•———

Stand Your Ground

Wouldn't it be wonderful to know that you were totally secure and not vulnerable to any attack of Satan? We know how bold he can be—why, he'll barge right in your life without even bothering to knock!

Some people believe that Christians never have struggles—but that's a lie. Satan's not just trying to destroy God's kingdom or the local church—he's after individual believers and their loved ones too! If you haven't taken the precautions for guarding yourself or those you love against Satan's divisive elements, you won't withstand the force of his storms—you will crash.

When God said, "My people are destroyed for lack of knowledge:..." (Hosea 4:6), I believe He had individual believers and our loved ones in mind. Sure, many powerful, demonic forces are contributing to the attacks that come against us, but God did *not* say that we would be destroyed by demonic forces.

Satan is taking advantage of us today because we have fallen prey to one of his most subtle devices—our own lack of knowledge. Paul wrote, "Lest Satan should get an advantage of us: for we are not ignorant of his devices" (2 Corinthians 2:11).

I want to teach you how to Satan-proof your life, your home, and your loved ones so that the next time the devil comes near you, you'll know how to stop him dead in his tracks!

Build a Solid Foundation

Of course, you cannot effectively stand against the devil on behalf of your loved ones until you have laid the right foundation for Satan-proofing yourself:

Therefore whosoever heareth these sayings of mine, and doeth them, I will liken him unto a wise man, which built his house upon a rock: And the rain descended, and the floods came, and the winds blew, and beat upon that house; and it fell not: for it was founded upon a rock. And every one that heareth these sayings of mine, and doeth them not, shall be likened unto a foolish man, which built his house upon the sand: And the rain descended, and the floods came, and the winds blew, and beat upon that house; and it fell: and great was the fall of it.

Matthew 7:24-29

Your foundation must be built upon a rock. The Bible says that Jesus Christ is the Rock of our salvation:

And did all drink the same spiritual drink: for they all drank of that spiritual Rock that followed them: and that Rock was Christ.

1 Corinthians 10:4

He shall cry unto me, Thou art my father, my God, and the rock of my salvation.

Psalms 89:26

I receive hundreds of letters each week from people all over the country. Many people write to share the terrible consequences of putting their confidence in something or someone other than Jesus Christ.

One courageous woman shared:

I was hooked on crack and walked the streets of Daytona Beach collecting aluminum cans to pay for my habit. I lived with crooks, thieves, *and prostitutes; and I was all of these. I am an educated woman with a master's degree, and I once had held a $50,000-a-year job. But I did not know Jesus—cocaine was my choice.*

Cocaine had become this woman's god, and it almost destroyed her. She eventually was born again, returned to her parents' home, and God began to nurture her back to spiritual health. She had taken the first step to Satan-proofing her life, and she became a dynamite witness to her family. Since her first letter, her older brother also has been set free from a drug-induced lifestyle. He now lives with her, and they are praising the Lord together.

Friend, there absolutely is no question. If you put your hope into anything or anyone less than Jesus, you are building your future on sand and you will fall into destruction.

Structured by the Word

After your eternal life has been established solidly in Christ Jesus, the next step toward Satan-proofing yourself and your loved ones is to structure your life on the godly principles contained in God's Word.

My ministry magazine, *Outpouring*, has a Bible-reading plan that is excellent! We receive many testimonies from all kinds of people who have been blessed because they are reading through the Bible each year. My heart was so touched when a teenage girl wrote:

I think it is beneficial for teenagers to read through the Bible. When I first started, it was like I had to make myself read it every day. But once I had established it as a discipline, then it got easier. I don't expect some big revelation every day; I just try to understand what it's really saying …and stick with it because in the long run, it will pay off.

This delightful believer's faith has been founded in Jesus Christ, and now she is Satan-proofing herself by studying the Bible. When she is confronted by temptations or trials, her response will be structured by God's Word.

You know, it's curious that *both* the houses discussed in Matthew 7 were subjected to the same type of storm. I know some believers think that their lives automatically became immune to the attacks of the enemy when they were born again. Others think their level of spirituality determines whether or not they are attacked by the devil. But it simply isn't so.

Of course, being a mature Christian certainly will give you a tremendous edge over the devil. But the simple fact remains that whether you are a saint or a sinner, a new Christian or a mature believer—Satan will throw his fiery darts at you. Why? Satan hates God; therefore, he also hates people because we were created in God's image.

> *So God created man in his own image, …and God said unto them, Be fruitful and multiply, and replenish the earth, and subdue it: . . .*
>
> Genesis 1:27,28

The Hebrew word here for *subdue* means "to tread down, to conquer, to bring into bondage."[1] It's God's will for people to bear fruit and to control the earth. But first, we must renew our minds and be conformed to the image of Christ (see Romans 8:29).

The major thing you will discover as you study your Bible is that Jesus is a winner. And, when you structure your life upon the godly principles that He taught in the Scriptures, *you* will become a winner too!

In Christ, believers have the power to tread over the devil:

> *Behold, I give unto you power to tread on serpents and scorpions, and over all the power of the enemy: and nothing shall by any means hurt you.*
>
> Luke 10:19

In Christ, believers are more than conquerors:

> *Nay, in all these things we are more than conquerors through him that loved us.*
>
> Romans 8:37

In Christ, believers have the authority to bind and loose:

> *Verily I say unto you, Whatsoever ye shall bind on earth shall be bound in heaven: and whatsoever ye shall loose on earth shall be loosed in heaven.*
>
> Matthew 18:18

When you begin to walk fully according to the purpose and in the power given to you by God, you will be able to Satan-proof yourself and keep the devil from ripping off your loved ones.

You'll learn to stop listening to the devil's lies! God does not want your marriage to end prematurely because of the death of your spouse or because of divorce. God does not want your family members tormented in relationships that are physically, mentally, emotionally, or sexually abusive. God does not want or your loved ones to fall into sin and become hooked on drugs and alcohol, adultery, pornography, or just plain "riotous living." God does not want your finances to be in such turmoil that you have to work day and night to make ends meet. *No,* He most certainly does not!

God has predestined you, His child, to be conformed into the image of Jesus. (See Romans 8:29.) Remember, Jesus is a winner; and through Him, you can be a winner too!

Although the enemy will try to conquer you, you can stop him from devastating you and Satan-proof your life by taking a stand on the Word of God.

Step Into the Battle Zone

I noticed something about those two houses in Matthew. This first house was Satan-proofed—rooted in Jesus and structured in God's Word, while the second house was built on sand (something or someone other than Christ and solid Bible doctrine). Both houses were subjected to the *same* storm; but although the first house may have swayed and bent under the ferocity of the winds and rains—it did not fall.

And the rain descended, and the floods came, and the winds blew, and beat upon that house; and it fell not: for it was founded upon a rock.

Matthew 7:25

In contrast, the second house had not been Satan-proofed; it had been built on sand. It couldn't handle the pressure of the storm and was destroyed. Since God wants us (and our loved ones) to be Satan-proofed, let's dig deeper into what it takes to be a Satan-proofer.

We know without a doubt that being born again is essential and reading the Bible is necessary. But knowing Jesus as our Savior and being aware of godly principles are simply the first steps toward defending ourselves and our loved ones against Satan's tactics.

Satan-proofers are believers who have taken charge by letting godly principles become alive in their circumstances. They have stepped out of the comfort zone of merely hearing God's Word, into the battle zone of actively doing what God's Word instructs us to do:

But be ye doers of the word, and not hearers only, deceiving your own selves.

James 1:22

The Bible gives us much more than the steps to eternal life; it also provides step-by-step instructions for living in the world every day. When you really get into studying your Bible regularly, you'll be able to Satan-proof your life as you begin to act on the Word of God that is within you. Some people read the Bible over and over again, but fail to apply its divine principles to their everyday lives. The Word has worked for people since biblical times, and the Word will work in your twenty-first century life too!

In order to take a stand upon godly principles, a believer first needs to have developed a trusting relationship with God. Then when the storms of life come, a Satan-proofer says, "God, I trust You; and I'm going to stand on what Your Word says. I know You are faithful, and You will not fail me."

This type of intimacy between God and man evolves out of a strong, consistent prayer life. A Satan-proofer regularly spends time in God's presence praying, worshiping, praising, fasting, studying the Word, and meditating on it. A Satan-proofer knows and trusts God to the utmost.

Your relationship with God, based on the rock-solid foundation of Jesus Christ, is what always will hold you steady as you are battling the enemy for yourself and others.

Standing in the Gap

Satan-proofing your loved ones requires you to be a gap stander. When I think about standing in the gap for my loved ones, I think about Abraham—

he spent time in God's presence; and God established a personal relationship with Abraham. I get so encouraged when I look at the relationship between Abraham and God; it was so intimate. The Bible indicates that God even trusted Abraham enough to reveal His plans regarding the coming judgment upon the wicked twin cities of Sodom and Gomorrah:

> *And the LORD said, Shall I hide from Abraham that thing which I do; ...Because the cry of Sodom and Gomorrah is great, and because their sin is very grievous; I will go down now, and see whether they have done altogether according to the cry of it, which is come unto me; and if not, I will know.*
>
> Genesis 18:17, 20-21

These people really were the pits! They were involved in all kinds of things—terrible sexual sins. Some of those awful Sodomite men even demanded that Lot turn over to them the two angels that God had sent to confirm their wicked activities. They wanted to have sex with God's angels—say "*yuk*"! So God said, "That's enough!" And He destroyed them.

Abraham began to Satan-proof his loved ones through intercessory prayer.

But prior to that, we see God actually conferring with Abraham about His plans to bring judgment upon Sodom and Gomorrah. How did Abraham react? Certainly he was concerned because his nephew Lot and Lot's family lived in Sodom.

Let's see, did Abraham go running to tell Sarah about what God was going to do? Did Abraham start whining to his friends, "Oh, what shall I do? Something awful is going to happen; please pray for my family"? Did Abraham get nervous and start biting his nails or pulling out his hair?

No! Abraham began to talk with God on behalf of Lot and his family. Abraham began to Satan-proof his loved ones through intercessory prayer: "Peradventure there be fifty righteous within the city: wilt thou also destroy and not spare the place for the fifty righteous that are therein? ...And the LORD said, If I find in Sodom fifty righteous within the city, then I will spare all the place for their sakes" (Genesis 18:24,26).

Abraham kept right on negotiating until God agreed to spare the city even if there were only ten righteous people living in it. Can you imagine, these people were so wicked that it was questionable as to whether Sodom contained ten good people?

I think Abraham probably stopped at ten because he thought there had to be at least ten good people in Sodom. After all, there were six in Lot's family—his wife, two daughters, and their husbands. Surely God would find four more people who had not been overtaken by the terrible sin that was running rampant in that area. Abraham had no idea that Lot's two sons-in-law would reject God's offer or that Lot's wife would turn from God too.

I wonder how I would respond if God suddenly said, "Marilyn, because of the homosexuality, prostitution, and drug abuse in Anywhere, USA; I am going to wipe it off the face of the earth." How would you respond? Some Christians probably would cheer God on and say, "Go ahead, God! We need to get some of these sinners out of here!" But what if you had relatives living in that city; would you feel the same way?

No matter how terrible the place, I believe God would expect us to be merciful and try to save the city if for no other reason than our families are there.

I believe prayer is one way the wise woman in Proverbs 14:1 stood in the gap and Satan-proofed her home. On the other hand, the foolish woman plucked her house down with her own hands. Do you suppose that instead of praying, she just pointed her finger at everyone's mistakes while her family crumbled under the weight of Satan's attacks?

Most Christians have allowed themselves to become foolish by pointing a finger rather than pointing a prayer. And while we busily have been focusing on the greatness of sin instead of the greatness of God—the devil merrily has been running off with everything we hold dear.

But I want to encourage you because there is hope! It is not too late for Christians to take a stand against the destruction the devil has planned for us or those we love.

God is for us! (Romans 8:31.) He doesn't want you or your loved ones to be destroyed by any of the horrendous things that come out of the devil's devious mind. No, God wants you to become an intercessor and to Satan-proof those you love with effective, fervent prayer.

You see, God is omniscient (all-knowing). God knew before He ever shared His plans with Abraham that he would stand in the gap and Satan-proof Lot's family. It didn't matter to Abraham that Lot was a loser, he prayed for him anyway. That's why God allows you to know some "not so nice" things about your loved ones too. He doesn't want you to point your finger and condemn; instead, God wants you to pray and stop what the devil is trying to do to them.

It's up to us to pray for our loved ones—to keep them before God. Who is going to do it if we don't? You may say, "Well, I think the Church should." But God wants *you* to stand in the gap for your own family and others.

I just love the way God works when He has gap standers willing to Satan-proof their loved ones.

Abraham could have chosen to be a gap finder and said, "I didn't want Lot to move down there, but he insisted. And Lot didn't just stay out on the plains where he had pitched his tent; he does all his shopping in Sodom, that's where his girls go to school, and he and his wife have an active social life. Why, Lot even sits at the city gate with the other civic leaders. You know, God, he may be family; but Lot really is not so swift. So go ahead and wipe Sodom out. I'll understand." Of course, we know Abraham didn't say any of that; instead, he stood in the gap and Satan-proofed Lot and his family with prayer. Abraham didn't think God was going to destroy Sodom and Gomorrah, so imagine how his faith fell when he got up the next morning:

And he looked toward Sodom and Gomorrah, and toward all the land of the plain, and beheld, and, lo, the smoke of the country went up as the smoke of a furnace.

Genesis 19:28

When Abraham saw all that smoke rising, I'm sure he probably thought, *Oh dear God, dear God, what about Lot? You couldn't find even ten?* Then, sadly,

Abraham got discouraged because the outward manifestations of God's answer to his prayer weren't quite what he expected them to be.

It's so easy to become discouraged when we pray and pray for our loved ones but nothing seems to change. My husband and I have been praying for our relatives for years. Some of them have gotten better, and some of them have gone from bad to worse. But we are going to keep on praying because God's Word has been formed on the inside of us, and we are holding on to His promises. Abraham let go of God's promises and completely blew it:

And Abraham journeyed from thence toward the south country, and dwelled between Kadesh and Shur, and sojourned in Gerar. And Abraham said of Sarah his wife, She is my sister: and Abimelech king of Gerar sent, and took Sarah. But God came to Abimelech in a dream by night and said to him, Behold thou art but a dead man, for the woman which thou has taken; for she is a man's wife.

Genesis 20:1-3

Abraham was afraid that Lot had been killed. Now, I am sure that you have gotten out of whack, too, when things didn't turn out as you thought they should. I certainly have, and like Abraham, I tried to back away from God's plan for my life.

Abraham had gotten out of God's will and into fear. He ended up telling Sarah to lie about being his wife and almost got poor Abimelech killed. Things really got pretty messy for a while until God corrected the situation and put Abraham back on the right track. But if Abraham had not judged God's faithfulness according to his own agenda, he never would have become discouraged and taken this dumb detour down to Gerar anyway.

When we are Satan-proofing our loved ones, it is important that we not become discouraged and give up just because things don't progress the way we think they should. We have to stick to the Word and believe that God will work His will out in whatever situation they are facing.

And don't forget the wise woman in Proverbs 14:1—build up rather than tear down. If you keep in mind that the devil is your enemy—never people—

you'll never tear your loved ones apart. Rather, you'll always zero in on Satan and tear him apart instead.

Years ago, before my children were born, my husband, Wally, was severely depressed. He became moody, he wouldn't talk to me sometimes for two or three days. I just hated it. I would try to talk to him; but he would say, "I'm a failure. Please don't talk to me; don't bother me."

I honestly didn't know what to do; but I heard the Word of God that had formed on the inside of me—that the Holy Spirit will pray for things beyond your understanding. I thought, "I'm going to stop whining around and being mad at Wally. I have the Word inside me, and I am going to act like the Word works by taking a stand on it."

So for one hour I prayed in tongues, and God showed me what to do. I sat down and began to go through the Scriptures with Wally, reminding him that he could not possibly be a failure because the Bible says that believers will always triumph in Christ.

First Wally just wanted me to leave him alone, but I continued challenging him and insisting that he respond. Finally, he started to laugh and the depression broke. That was over twenty years ago, and Wally hasn't been severely depressed since.

I stood in the gap and Satan-proofed my loved ones by acting on God's Word inside of me. I spoke the Word, and the devil had to stop attacking my husband with depression.

Wield the Sword

The Bible says that God's Word is a sword:

And take the helmet of salvation, and the sword of the Spirit, which is the word of God.

Ephesians 6:17

For the word of God is quick, and powerful, and sharper than any twoedged sword, piercing even to the dividing asunder of soul and spirit, and of the joints and marrow, and is a discerner of the thoughts and intents of the heart.

Hebrews 4:12

Someone once told me about a Spirit-filled man whom I'll call Tom. He had been praying for his sister who was hooked on drugs and involved in all kinds of immorality. She lived a very sinful life. One weekend, while their mother was away, the sister went out and didn't come home until 6:30 the next morning. She brought some athletic-looking guy home with her, and they went into her mother's bedroom.

Tom was almost overwhelmed when he asked God what to do, and God told him, "Throw the guy out!" He went into his mother's bedroom, told his sister to put her clothes on, and asked her boyfriend, "How would you feel if your sister brought some guy home to sleep with her in your mother's bed? Would you like it?" The boyfriend responded, "No." Tom told him to get dressed and leave, and the guy did just that. His sister absolutely was furious.

When Tom left and returned to school, he began to Satan-proof his sister. He stood in the gap and spoke *for* his sister saying, "Satan, you can't have any part of my sister. Adultery, you can't have a part of my sister. Drugs, you can't have a part of my sister." Tom continued this for exactly three months, and one day his sister showed up at his door saying, "I want to get saved." The Word of God had cut through all the junk in her life and had turned her completely around!

God's Word discerns the thoughts and intents of the heart. So when we pray God's Word, using it on demonic spirits and situations, it begins to cut through thoughts and attitudes and brings about a change.

Instead of complaining and allowing corrupt communication (see Ephesians 4:29) to come out of our mouths about how badly people are doing, we literally need to speak to their spirit—by name—"Susie (or whoever), you're not going to drink or take drugs." And then, Satan-proof them by speaking directly to the enemy, "Devil, you're not going to put alcoholism and drug addiction on Susie" (or whomever).

I believe when we begin to speak and continue to speak with persistence like that, we will crack some things wide open. Why? Because our foundation is in Jesus—the living Word. The Bible says that we overcome the devil by the blood of the Lamb and the word of our testimony. (See Revelation 12:11.) We can Satan-proof our loved ones by cutting through some of the garbage in their lives so they can hear the Holy Spirit in their hearts; then they will come through with flying colors!

So you see, it's more than just knowing Jesus and being aware of what God's Word says. A Satan-proofer literally takes the Word and chops off the devil's head with it.

Why don't you begin *now* to be wise like the woman in Proverbs 14:1 and build up your loved ones through intercessory prayer?

A Satan-proofer literally takes the Word and chops off the devil's head with it.

For instance, I believe that women can Satan-proof their husbands by speaking the Word over their husband's clothes while ironing them or over the sheets on their bed: "I thank You, Father, because no weapon formed against my husband shall prosper; and everything that rises against him shall fall." I think something happens in a home when women pray like that; they can prevent violent crimes from occurring in their home and they can put strife on the run!

Men can Satan-proof their wives by speaking to their spirits, "Mary (or whoever), you will never be a nag. You will always be sweet because you have the peace of God that passes all understanding." Speak God's Word concerning obedience into your children's spirits—tell them they will never be rebellious and how smart they are in school because they have the mind of Christ. And then speak with authority to the devil; tell him that he will never get your loved ones because, in the name of Jesus, *you* are standing in the gap for them.

Finally, I cannot emphasize enough the importance of praying in the Holy Spirit. The Bible says:

> *But ye, beloved, building up yourselves on your most holy faith, praying in the Holy Ghost, keep yourselves in the love of God, looking for the mercy of our Lord Jesus Christ unto eternal life.*

> Jude 20-21

Now let me ask you, what do you think would happen if you began to walk around your house praying in the Spirit, or on your job? You don't have to make a big fuss, you can pray in the Spirit on the inside—no one would know what you are doing but God.

Praying in the Spirit will keep you in the love of God, and I believe praying in the Spirit also will keep you in love with each other. So when your spouse, your children, your parents, or other loved ones get out of line; you will lovingly pray and Satan-proof them. The Holy Spirit will keep you in God's perfect love, and you will act in a way that will bring God's mercy into whatever situation Satan may try to bring against your lives.

CHAPTER 5

Lifting Up a Standard

When you become a bona fide Satan-proofer, you will need the power of God because what you actually are doing is declaring war on Satan. You're saying, "No!" to the destructive plans he has concocted to bring division and strife into your life and your relationships. In order to succeed at stopping the devil, it is imperative that you are moving in the power of the Holy Spirit; so as we continue to look at practical steps to being a Satan-proofer, I am going to put a lot of emphasis upon that.

We need to be led by the Holy Spirit because, in case you haven't noticed, there is a lot of stress in life. I'm sure you've heard that old saying, "The boss strikes out at you, you go home and strike out at your spouse, your spouse strikes out at the kids, and the kids strike out at the poor dog!" Even though this sounds humorous, that's basically what often happens.

We may not intentionally want to hurt someone we love; nevertheless, we tend to strike out and hurt those who are closest to us. However, when they have been Satan-proofed by the presence of the Holy Spirit and your boss gets on your nerves, instead of taking it out on someone else, the Holy Spirit will help you work out your emotional frustrations before you cause trouble for your loved ones.

So what do you do when someone strikes out at you? You pray (without letting anyone else hear you) in the Holy Spirit, and God will help you to respond to others in love—even when they are being very unloving toward you. You'll find that your life will be a lot less stressful if you Satan-proof your relationships by allowing the Holy Spirit to lead you in them.

For example, if you have children, one of the first things the Holy Spirit will lead you to do concerning your children is to raise them to serve God. Do you remember what God said about Abraham? "He will command his children and his household after him..." (Genesis 18:19).

God was saying that Abraham would raise his children to serve the Lord. God must have had a lot of confidence in Abraham because these words were spoken before Abraham and Sarah's child was even born. That's quite a compliment; certainly the best one Abraham ever received. What about your household? What does God say about your child rearing techniques? Does He say that you are raising your children up to serve Him?

Maybe you raised your children according to God's Word; but they still went the way of the world and fell into a destructive lifestyle. I understand how you feel; my son got involved in drugs. But I raised him to serve the Lord, and I refuse to measure the truth of God's Word according to my son's lifestyle. I know that my son, Michael's, life is going to line up with what God says about him. The Bible says it, and I believe it with all my heart.

Parents are supposed to plant the seed of God's Word into the hearts of their children. We teach them the Bible and keep them exposed to a godly lifestyle. But as far as serving the Lord is concerned, that only happens when their hearts have been changed, and that involves a work of the Holy Spirit.

After Abraham had commanded his children to serve God, the Bible says they kept the way of God:

> *...they shall keep the way of the LORD, to do justice and judgment; that the LORD may bring upon Abraham that which he hath spoken of him.*
>
> Genesis 18:19

Why did they continue to serve God? Because Abraham had planted God's Word into their hearts, and the Spirit of the Lord caused them to obey God after they had grown up.

You may not know it, but you can't force your children to obey God, especially when they are out of your sight. Obedience to God comes out of the heart. So even though Abraham's children may have started out obeying God simply because it was a household rule, after they grew up and developed a personal relationship with God for themselves, they obeyed God because they loved Him. There is a lot of tension between many parents and their children. But the Holy Spirit drew Isaac unto God, and the Holy Spirit will draw your child also:

Train up a child in the way he should go: and when he is old, he will not depart from it.

Proverbs 22:6

That reminds me of one time when we got a letter that was so touching from a prisoner who had gotten hold of my book, *A Cry for Miracles*. He said he was a Victnam War veteran and had been experiencing terrible conflict because he had killed people during the war. As a child he had been taught in Sunday school that it was wrong to kill. After the war his wife and daughter were drowned in a boating accident. This was so tragic. His letter said he just couldn't take any more, and he simply "lost it." He became addicted to drugs, began to write phony prescriptions for codeine, and eventually he ended up in prison:

I just thought there was no hope for me…I had been in despair until I read that book. Out of the blackness of where I was, I began to see a little pinpoint of light.

His letter was full of hope, and he intended to go to the prison chaplain and ask for prayer. When I read his letter, I thought, *Wow, somebody way back in his Lutheran background got the Word into him and probably prayed for him.* They had Satan-proofed this man as a child; and although he had detoured and suffered through so many terrible experiences, that precious seed had taken root and was now beginning to sprout.

61

Friend, we are to bring our children up according to God's Word. And, by faith, we must know that God will manifest His will in their lives despite what outward circumstances may look like.

We Christians begin to Satan-proof our children when we dedicate them in church and bring them to Sunday school. When we do that, I believe that God's supernatural hand comes upon our children. And then God dispatches angels to go before and behind our children not only to protect them, but also to cause their lives to stay in line with His Word.

So what if everything doesn't turn out the way we think it should in our children's lives! There will come a time when God's all-powerful Holy Spirit will draw our children to God through Jesus Christ. I have watched it happen again and again.

Third Member of the Trinity

By now you may be wondering, "Who is the Holy Spirit, where is the Holy Spirit, and how can I be instructed by the Holy Spirit?"

Know ye not that ye are the temple of God, and that the Spirit of God dwelleth in you?

1 Corinthians 3:16

The Holy Spirit is the third member of the Trinity along with the Father and the Son. The Holy Spirit is God; and if you are a born-again believer, the Holy Spirit lives inside your spirit.

There are many names in the Bible that describe different attributes of God. One of them is El Shaddai, which means "the God who is more than enough." Job really got a revelation of El Shaddai because when Job had lost his family, his health, and his wealth, the God who was more than enough restored everything to Job in double portion (see Job 42:12). Abraham and Sarah encountered El Shaddai when the God who is more then enough opened Sarah's barren womb, and she conceived Isaac despite the fact that they were long past the childbearing age (see Genesis 21:1-3).

The Holy Spirit is the Spirit of God who is more than enough, and He has made Himself available to you. When you don't have the answers for the many, many circumstances that come against you and your loved ones, just remember the Spirit of the living God is waiting with fail-proof instructions to direct you through any situation coming your way.

If you have the Holy Spirit, you have the Instructor.

How does He instruct you? Sometimes God will give you visions—I haven't had very many visions, probably about three that I can recall; but they were wonderful. Most of the instructions that I've received from the Holy Spirit have come like impressions from deep in my spirit. But sometimes the Holy Spirit will instruct you with a Scripture, and your answer will become clearer to you as you meditate on God's Word.

There are many Scriptures that exhort believers to allow the Holy Spirit to instruct them. You might be thinking, *Well, I'm just not very spiritual. I haven't read through the entire Bible; I don't pray in tongues two or three hours a day. I don't get very excited, and I don't dance or even clap my hands during worship.*

But the Bible doesn't say you have to do all of that to be led by the Holy Spirit; so don't try to build up some kind of case with requirements that are too hard for you to handle. The bottom line is that if you've been born again, you're the temple. If you're the temple, you have the Holy Spirit. If you have the Holy Spirit, you have the Instructor. If you have the Instructor, He can do the work of El Shaddai in your situation. It's that easy, so don't try and make things difficult for yourself.

Another way the Holy Spirit will instruct you is through unctions. An unction is "a special endowment, an anointing"[1]:

> *But ye have an unction from the Holy One, and ye know all things.*
>
> 1 John 2:20

The Holy Spirit has given believers a special anointing to know all things. I know, some days you may not feel so smart; but within you is the potential to know all things. I think that's marvelous, especially on the days when I don't feel too swift. It's comforting to know that no matter how tough a situation we may be facing, the Holy Spirit will teach us how to Satan-proof ourselves and our loved ones and keep the devil from doing any damage to them while we are dealing with the crisis.

I was on a plane to Atlanta, and one of the flight attendants (I'll call her Rachel) told me she was born again and Spirit-filled. Rachel was unsure as to whether or not she should continue in her profession because sometimes she was required to serve liquor to the passengers. Then she told me about an incident when a man became drunk and began to act very crudely toward the women on the airplane. Rachel started praying in the Spirit and asked God for a revelation on how to handle this man.

The Holy Spirit directed her to go and sit next to the intoxicated man. While she sat there praying quietly, pretty soon the man's hand was on her leg. Rachel moved his hand and said, "I know you have a wonderful wife at home who is praying for you, and you're just living and acting like a dog! What is wrong with you?"

Well, the man was just stunned; and he asked, "How did you know my wife is a Christian and she prays in tongues?" Rachel continued to blast him, "You're a lecherous, lustful man, and I'm going to cast those evil spirits out of you right now"! She did, and the man was set free; and he gave his life to the Lord right there on that airplane.

There were two things working here that I want you to see. First, what was the man's wife doing? She was Satan-proofing her home by praying in the Spirit. How do you think he ended up on that particular flight? It was the Holy Spirit. And then the Holy Spirit gave Rachel a special anointing to handle this specific situation.

You may not agree; but I don't believe we can put God in a box and tell Him how, where, or when to use people. I certainly am not advocating Christians to be involved in a sinful lifestyle. But I know that Satan is gaining hold of one precious soul after another because believers have been content to stay hidden away in comfortable church buildings instead of doing what God intended—subduing the earth!

When Rachel, the flight attendant, mentioned her dilemma about her job again, this time the Holy Spirit gave me an unction. I reminded Rachel of Nehemiah, who was the cupbearer to Artaxerxes, the king of Persia. The Bible says the cup contained wine (see Nehemiah 2:1). So if God could use Nehemiah despite the fact that he served liquor, He surely could continue to use Rachel too.

What Happens When You Pray?

Remember earlier how we talked about Satan-proofing our relationships by praying in the Holy Spirit (see Jude 1:20-21)? Now I want to tell you some very practical things concerning how you treat your family members and others, so you'll know exactly what happens when you pray in the Holy Spirit.

I believe praying in the Spirit gives us a special anointing to love people who maybe aren't so lovable at that particular time. Let's be honest; it's not easy to keep loving someone who says all kinds of terrible things that cut you to your heart and hurt you deeply. But if you want to keep the devil out of your relationships, you'll have to pray in the Holy Spirit, and God will build you up in those hurting places. God will help you to keep focused on His wonderful love instead of focusing on the offenses, hurts, wounds, or defeats that the devil will try to intensify in your heart.

Let's talk about knowledge for a moment:

...we know that we all have knowledge. Knowledge puffeth up, but charity edifieth.

1 Corinthians 8:1

We all can know how to treat people. There are thousands of "how-to" books and articles available that will give you step-by-step directions to develop a fulfilling relationship with your spouse, your children, and others you care for. But it is apparent that this type of knowledge is not working for a lot of Christians. Division, disagreement, gossip, and criticism continue to sweep through the Church. This is because many believers are not being Satan-proofers by praying in the Holy Spirit. Most of us are not encouraging ourselves in the love of God concerning our families and other loved ones. Instead, we only are gathering knowledge, and knowledge without love has thrown believers into a tremendous pride level.

Many Christians have elevated themselves so high in the vast knowledge available on how to construct healthy relationships that they have become very mechanical in their thinking. People in this kind of pride don't enjoy people—they don't enjoy their children, their spouse, or anyone else. There is no godly love operating here, but only a feeling of having to be the "expert" or always having to know the correct way to do everything. I think it's boring to be with someone who knows everything all the time. Even if they were right all the time, I wouldn't want to be around them.

As a pastor's wife, I have heard this complaint so many times. Your relationships will function so much better if you don't try to be the one to know everything. And if you do have to know everything, be sure that the first thing you know is all about godly love. This is not the emotional feeling that comes over us from time to time, but the real action of loving—the doing of beneficial things for those with whom we come into contact. You'll only discover this kind of love by spending time praying in the Holy Spirit. Then you'll take His instructions and Satan-proof those in your life by encouraging, building up, and edifying them in God's love.

You may be facing a situation today with someone that looks like death is lurking around. Remember that God always has brought life into dead situations through the power of the Holy Spirit. Look at Genesis 1:1-2—before the creation the earth was in such turmoil, confusion, and havoc. The Spirit of God brooded over the earth and turned chaos (confusion) into cosmos (order). When you start praying in tongues, the Holy Spirit will brood over your job, your loved ones, your household; and He will bring forth life and divine order where there may have been death and confusion. When we pray in the Holy Spirit, we bring life into our situations:

It is the spirit that quickeneth; the flesh profiteth nothing: the words that I speak unto you, they are spirit, and they are life.

John 6:63

Try it. If you are at home, just begin to walk through your house praying in the Spirit. Pray over your couch; over the kitchen chairs. Husbands and wives can pray over the bed together. Pray over each other's clothes, "Lord, let the person who wears these shoes walk in the life of the Holy Spirit."

I pray over my household all the time. My husband is a pastor, and I always pray over his pillow and over his clothes. When my daughter Sarah was in school, sometimes I would walk into her room and pray over her bed—asking God to give her special wisdom. I also would ask the Holy Spirit to give her life because I know how students like to stay up so late. I believe that God quickened her mind and her body so she could comprehend and learn better during the day.

Praying in the Spirit is like a thirsty man taking a long drink of water. The more you pray in the Spirit, the thirstier you will become; and the thirstier you become, the more you will pray. It's like a circle.

Take Your Stand

In order to Satan-proof our life and our loved ones, there must be a standard lifted up against the devil. This comes about when believers become involved in intercessory prayer:

For he put on righteousness as a breastplate, and an helmet of salvation upon his head; and he put on the garments of vengeance for clothing, and was clad with zeal as a cloke

Isaiah 59:17

Wow! That's the armor of God; quite an outfit isn't it? So you say, "I'm going to be a Satan-proofer through intercessory prayer." Okay, when you put on *the breastplate of righteousness*, you'll begin to be bolder because you'll be walking in God's righteousness and not your own. *The helmet of salvation* will protect your mind from thoughts the devil would like you to think. Now the devil will still bring destructive thoughts to you. He'll tell you things like you are a failure, your spouse doesn't love you, your children are the pits, your friends don't really like you—but you don't have to dwell on that kind of junk because your mind is protected by the helmet of salvation.

What does all this sound like? It sounds to me as if someone is preparing for battle! These are battle clothes. You may say, "But Marilyn, I'm not going to be out on the mission fields or in evangelism fighting to further the gospel. I'm just going to be praying in my bedroom for the people I love." Then your bedroom will become a battlefield. That's where you are going to take your stand and tell the devil that he cannot have your marriage, your children, your relatives or friends, your finances, your future—or anything else that pertains to you!

When you put on the *garment of vengeance*, God says that He will repay the devil when he comes to your door trying to wreak havoc in your life:

According to their deeds, accordingly he will repay, fury to his adversaries, recompense to his enemies …When the enemy shall come in like a flood, the Spirit of the Lord shall lift up a standard against him.

Isaiah 59:18,19

The word *standard* here means "something that causes something else to vanish, flit, flee."[2] James 4:7 says, "Submit yourselves therefore to God. Resist the devil, and he will flee from you."

Once you have clothed yourself in the armor of God, then *you*, the intercessor, are the standard that God wants to lift up. Through the power of Christ Jesus, God wants you to resist the devil not only for yourself, but on behalf of your loved ones. And when you have submitted your life and have begun to develop a more intimate relationship with God, the devil will flee from you and those you pray for when you command it in Jesus' name. God wants you to Satan-proof your life, your family, and other loved ones by becoming such a tremendous intercessor that the devil won't want to waste his time on any of you!

CHAPTER 6

Living in the Overflow

I think it's important to explain to you that Satan-proofing your life and relationships is not just a "one-shot deal." I say this because you may be someone who will only put into action one of the principles outlined in this book, and you'll think you're safe. Then when the devil interrupts your life again, you'll say, "Hey, Marilyn, it didn't work!" But it's not that the principles don't work; it's that they all work *together*.

Satan-proofing your life, loving relationships, and others with whom you have contact is a continuous and progressive lifestyle. It's similar to a puzzle. Receiving Christ as your personal Savior is one piece, reading your Bible is another piece, applying the Word of God to your own flesh and to your circumstances is a piece, praying in the Holy Spirit is a piece, and speaking forth God's blessings is yet another piece. If we put all these pieces into their proper place, pretty soon we'll have a clearer picture of the image in which God created us—His image, the original Satan-Proofer!

The Act of Blessing

I have noticed something special about a Satan-proofer: His or her life just seems to overflow with wonderful blessings from God. Did you know that God began to bless people immediately after He created us?

So God created man in his own image, in the image of God created he him; male and female created he them. And God blessed them....

Genesis 1:27,28

The Hebrew word used here for *blessed* means "to kneel."[1] God put Adam and Eve in a kneeling posture—a position of worship. Why? So He could begin to prosper them with children and give them control over the earth. Of course, we know they got out of the worshiping-God posture and into the worshiping-their-own-desires posture. They really blew it big time not only for themselves, but for everyone else as well.

So, we know that it's God's desire to bless His people. I don't mean to say that God is like Santa Claus and gives us gifts like good health, finances, or peace in our homes. These are not gifts, they are benefits that we receive when we keep ourselves in an attitude of worship—they are the results of living a blessed life.

When we begin to apply blessings to ourselves and our loved ones, we really are saying, "God, put my loved ones and myself in a posture of worship so we can receive the benefits that accompany being in an intimate relationship with You." Isn't that what you really want for your life and those you love? Of course it is; so when you think about Satan-proofing your life, remember that you need to speak abundant blessings upon your loved ones too. Also, remember that you must be living in an attitude of worship in order to speak blessings. Friend, we just cannot live a sinful lifestyle and expect to remain consecrated in the authority of God. It just doesn't work that way. In order to bless others, we must first be blessed ourselves.

Basically there are five promises implied in the word bless: to benefit, to make whole, to prosper, to make healthy, and to make wealthy. When you speak God's blessing, you are reminding God of His promises. You're saying, "Father, I remind You of Your promises to Your covenant children: to benefit us, to make us whole, to prosper us, and to make us healthy and wealthy."

If you want a Satan-proofed life, then begin to bless your loved ones and others. The act of blessing is not to be taken lightly, because when we believers mix faith with blessings, we cause God to move on His promises. So whatever circumstance you may be facing, begin to bless the people involved.

70

There are four areas where God wants His blessings to overflow in the lives of His people: in our circumstances, toward our enemies, toward the Lord, and in our homes.

Wouldn't you like to see God's blessings manifested in all of your circumstances? How about at your workplace? Perhaps you're experiencing difficulty because your boss favors another employee over you. You have become offended, and you want to jump up and quit. But have you considered that God may want you to stay there to be a conduit for Him to pour out blessings upon those people? Hang in there, and thank God for the job. Begin to bless your boss as well as the other employee. God will bless everyone involved and move on your behalf as well.

Another area where God wants to manifest His wonderful benefits is toward your enemies. Are you thinking, *Marilyn, that's where I blow it; I simply cannot bless my enemies?*

All right, let's take a closer look at our enemies. We know that our real enemy is the devil. We will discuss this in depth later on, but in terms of people, let's define our enemies as people who either knowingly or unknowingly allow themselves to be used by the devil for the purpose of harming us.

I believe most Christians probably would agree that murderers, robbers, rapists, and the like are our enemies—and certainly these people are dangerous. Yet, many believers have been injured by parents who have neglected or abused them. Some have mates who are thoughtless and cruel, or their mate has deserted them. Others have "best friends" who have begun repeating their deepest secrets! And still others may have been manipulated or hurt by another Christian. Do any of these apply to you?

There are two things that I want you to see in all these situations. Someone has been injured, and someone has been used as a tool by the devil. Certainly I am not making light of the personal suffering that you may have experienced at the hands of another person; but isn't the person who injured you really just a victim too? I believe Satan uses people against each other to carry out his diabolical schemes to steal, to kill, and to destroy God's people (see John 10:10).

Think about it the next time someone comes against you, and remember that a Satan-proofer can bless his or her enemies. Is it easy? *No!* But it can be done by a believer who lives in an attitude of worship, by someone who wants to see God's loving benefits manifested more fully in people's lives:

> *But I say unto you, Love your enemies, bless them that curse you, do good to them that hate you, and pray for them which despitefully use you, and persecute you.*

Matthew 5:44

God also wants to bless us in our relationship with Him: "Bless the LORD, O my soul: and all that is within me, bless his holy name. Who forgiveth all thine iniquities; who healeth all thy diseases" (Psalms 103:1,3).

God is blessed by our obedience and praise. He is blessed by our worship; and when we bless God, we create an environment in which the blessings of God can flourish in our lives.

Another area where God wants us to be blessed is in our homes. Given the choice, most of us would like to see God's benefits flow into the lives of our loved ones first.

You can bless your children all through the day (God's Word is not bound by time or distance). Speak each child's name and say, "God bless you in your school work." Bless your children especially after they have been disciplined. Go to your child and say, "You have been misbehaving, but I love you; and I am asking God to bless you." I believe that when you mix your faith with the blessing, you'll see an improvement in your child's behavior, attitude, and academic performance.

A woman on my staff has a 15-year-old daughter whose rebellious behavior affected her performance in school. The woman prayed and sought God's wisdom for the situation. Then she began to speak God's blessings into her daughter's life. As the mother became more aware of the need to speak words of encouragement rather than criticism, the daughter's attitude and academic performance began to improve.

We wives who want to Satan-proof our homes need to bless our husbands—even when they're grumpy or mean. If he hurts you with unkind words or actions, resist the urge to talk back or pout; instead, pray (to yourself) and speak God's blessings upon him. It's not easy; and some wives may think, *Marilyn, I can't bless my husband. I'd rather strangle him!* Nevertheless, you must bless him—even if you have to say, "God, I'm angry with my husband right now; but by faith I ask You to bless him." The same thing goes for husbands.

Take Your Priestly Position

Now let's look at what actually happens when we speak God's blessings. The Bible says that God instructed the priests to bless the children of Israel:

And the LORD spake unto Moses, saying, Speak unto Aaron and unto his sons, saying, On this wise ye shall bless the children of Israel....

Numbers 6:22,23

What happened when the Israelites were blessed? "And Moses and Aaron went into the tabernacle of the congregation, and came out, and blessed the people: and the glory of the LORD appeared unto all the people" (Leviticus 9:23).

When the priests blessed the people, God's glory appeared—blessings bring forth a manifestation of the glory of God. Are you thinking, *That was fine for ancient Israel, but where are the modern-day priests?* The Bible says that believers are kings and priests:

And from Jesus Christ, ...Unto him that loved us, and washed us from our sins in his own blood, And hath made us kings and priests unto God and his Father....

Revelation 1:5,6

Do you want to see God's glory manifested in your family, your place of employment, your church, the nation, and the world? Then you must take the authority given to you by Christ Jesus. You must begin to function as a priest to the people with whom you have contact, and start speaking God's blessings into their lives.

I pray and speak God's blessings over my family, ministry and partners, the United States, and the world. Friend, if we want to see God manifest His glory, then we have to stop whining about how bad things are, take our priestly position, and begin to Satan-proof this world!

The Bible clearly tells us the major duties of priests:

At that time the LORD separated the tribe of Levi, to bear the ark of the covenant of the LORD, to stand before the LORD to minister unto him, and to bless in his name, unto this day.

Deuteronomy 10:8

What was so important about the Ark of the Covenant? It contained the Ten Commandments (the way), the golden pot of manna (the truth), and Aaron's rod that budded (the life). The way, the truth, and the life—who is that? Of course, it's Jesus! (John 14:6) The Old Testament priests carried the Ark and those things inside were pictures of the real thing—Jesus!

> *We don't have to make any more sacrifices, because one drop of Christ's sinless blood took care of all the sins in the world.*

The Bible also says the priests ministered to God. That means they lived their lives in an attitude of worship. They absolutely could not be in God's presence without being consecrated. And then they blessed people in His name.

What does God want believers—priests—to do today? He wants us to take the love and authority of Jesus to the world. God wants us to live in an attitude of worship, and then He wants us to bless people in the name of Jesus.

One of the many benefits that God wants His people to receive is forgiveness. In order for the Israelites to receive forgiveness for their sins, the Old Testament priests had to offer blood sacrifices. I would have thought, *What a pain to have to kill an animal every time we blow it.* I am so glad that we have the New Covenant, which was established through the shed blood of Jesus Christ. We don't have to make any more sacrifices, because one drop of Christ's sinless blood took care of all the sins in the world.

And there's something else about blessings: In Deuteronomy 33:1 we see that Moses blessed the children of Israel before his death. Moses went on to prophesy over all of the tribes of Israel. The word *bless* also means "to pronounce good things."[2] What was Moses doing? He was pronouncing good things upon the Israelites.

What about you? Do you pronounce good things upon your children? Your spouse? Your relatives and friends? Do you declare that they are going to do well in their lives and in their relationships? Do you declare them to be winners in everything that they encounter? Begin to bless them and they won't be vulnerable to Satan's deceptions.

Blessing or Cursing?

Have you ever known someone whose life and circumstances obviously were being flooded with God's glory—but they didn't even know it? A man named Balak, the king of Moab, experienced this very thing.

The Bible tells us how Balak had become very nervous because the Israelites were passing through Moab on their way to the Promised Land. When Balak heard that they were camped in Moab, he became terrified. He had heard about how the Israelites had killed two Amorite kings, Sihon and Og, and had taken a huge land grant. (See Numbers 21:33-35; 22:2-3.)

Picture the Israelites—they were ex-slaves who had been in bondage for over 400 years, and they were totally untrained in warfare. Yet they had succeeded in conquering a land that no one else had been able to conquer. It was obvious to everyone that they had supernatural help from God. People were saying, "Did you hear what happened? Those Israelites got all that land when they overcame Sihon and Og. They did it because they worship some kind of God who blesses them!"

This was also frightening to the Perizzites, the Hivites, and all the rest of those "ites." Everyone panicked when they heard that the Israelites were coming. After all, Israel had a mighty God who had parted the Red Sea and had killed all those Egyptians—including Pharaoh! Then Israel's God had helped them kill Sihon and Og—two more kings.

So when Balak heard the Israelites were in his country, he naturally wondered, *Am I going to die next?* Poor Balak didn't realize that he and his people were blessed because God had commanded the Israelites not to harm them. Why? Because the Moabites were descendants of Abraham's nephew Lot, which made them shirttail relatives of the Israelites, who were direct descendants of Abraham.

Remember when Lot and his two daughters escaped the judgment on Sodom and went to live in a cave in the mountains? (See Genesis 19:30-37.) Well, Lot's daughters got him drunk and committed incest with him—*yuk, yuk!* The oldest daughter named her son Moab, and he became the father of the Moabites.

Despite the Moabites' bad beginning, God had blessed them and had told the Israelites not to harm them. But since Balak didn't know God and he did not know that the Israelites wouldn't harm the Moabites, he hired the prophet Balaam to curse Israel. Balaam tried and tried to curse the Israelites. He even climbed two different mountains and tried to curse them, but every time he opened his mouth, only blessings came forth. Finally, he said: "Behold, I have received commandment to bless: and he hath blessed; and I cannot reverse it" (Numbers 23:20).

Balaam was saying, "I cannot curse these people because they have God's blessings upon them—what God has blessed, no one can curse." What a startling revelation! And, friend, the same thing is true today.

When you begin to Satan-proof your relationships and circumstances by speaking forth the blessings from God, you can believe that no devilish curse can come against them!

Let me show you something about how problems with our loved ones and others are affected by the words we speak. You may think that Christians do not speak curses upon people, but what about the hateful, negative things we sometimes say to each other?

For instance, what happens when you come in from work and you say something unkind to your spouse: "You are so fat; when are you going to go on a diet!" Or, "You have bad breath and body odor—go brush your teeth and take a bath!" Or your poor children—how do you talk to them? Some parents are always speaking negatively, "You'll never amount to anything! Clean up that nasty room; you act just like a pig in a pigpen!"

Are we blessing or are we cursing? If you want the devil to steal your marriage, your family, your friendships just continue talking to each other in a negative manner.

I know of a young couple who was having some marital problems. One holiday, the wife gave her husband an ultimatum that he would either have to do things her way, or pack his things and get out!

The husband quickly recognized that the devil was trying to destroy his marriage. So instead of becoming angry, this young believer got out his blessed oil and began to anoint their property including the doors, the windows, the dresser drawers, and the driveway. The husband began to speak blessings on his wife and into their marriage. The couple is together today, and their marriage continues to grow in the Lord.

This young man had a choice, didn't he? He could have just thrown the doors to his marriage wide open and let Satan rob him blind. But instead, he Satan-proofed his household; and he spoke blessings upon his circumstances: "Blessings are upon the head of the just: but violence covereth the mouth of the wicked" (Proverbs 10:6).

Let me tell you about someone else who blessed his circumstances:

And Esau hated Jacob because of the blessing wherewith his father blessed him: and Esau said in his heart, The days of mourning for my father are at hand; then will I slay my brother Jacob.

Genesis 27:41

I would say that one brother hating another enough to want to kill him is a pretty serious situation, wouldn't you? Why did Esau hate Jacob? Because Jacob had received the firstborn blessing from their father, Isaac. As the oldest son, Esau was supposed to inherit the blessing; but he had become careless about spiritual things and had sold his birthright to Jacob for a bowl of stew. However, Esau was not the only one in the wrong; Jacob used a lot of trickery to get the blessing. Esau got so mad at Jacob that he threatened to kill him, but he never did. Why? God's blessings were upon Jacob, and what God had blessed could not be cursed.

When Rebekah found out that her son Esau wanted to kill his brother, she sent Jacob to live with her brother Laban (see Genesis 27:43). Before Jacob left, his father, Isaac, blessed him again (see Genesis 28:1-4). The Bible tells us that Jacob certainly prospered during the 14 years that he lived in Haran with his uncle Laban. Jacob married two of Laban's daughters, Leah and Rachel, and fathered 12 sons. Jacob also became wealthy:

> *And the man increased exceedingly, and had much cattle, and maidservants, and men-servants, and camels, and asses.*
>
> Genesis 30:43

Eventually Jacob returned from Haran to Canaan, and it's interesting to see how he treated Esau. Jacob knew that he could not avoid meeting Esau— I don't think Jacob was looking forward to seeing his brother at all. He knew that he had taken unfair advantage of his brother and that Esau had good reason to be upset.

So Jacob had an all-night prayer meeting, and God really dealt with him about his own attitude. When Jacob finally did encounter Esau, he didn't reopen the old wound. Instead, Jacob blessed Esau with gifts and allowed God to defuse that potentially explosive situation.

Friend, there is a simple truth working here that we need to get hold of: When we Satan-proof our circumstances by speaking forth God's blessings, we reap blessings. But speaking forth negative words only brings a curse.

Bless Each Other's Circumstances

God wants us to bless each other's circumstances too like Joshua blessed Caleb:

> *And Joshua blessed him, and gave unto Caleb the son of Jephunneh Hebron for an inheritance.*
>
> Joshua 14:13

Joshua had led the Israelites into the Promised Land, and now he was getting the people situated into the areas where they were supposed to settle.

Caleb had said, "Joshua, I want that piece of land that I claimed when we first came to Canaan as spies." So Joshua blessed Caleb and gave him the land he desired.

When we follow Caleb's life, we see that he was one of the most blessed men of God. And Caleb blessed his daughter Achsah even after she married and left his care. She ended up marrying a Spirit-filled man named Othniel, who later became the first judge in Israel.

In our day, it's relatively easy for young women to find Spirit-filled men to marry. But during those times, it was very unusual for people to become Spirit filled. So Achsah's marriage really was blessed, and Caleb had a lot to do with her circumstances.

I think Caleb was a very wise father. Sadly, many parents today want to get their children out of their homes quickly; and therefore, they aren't too concerned with whom their children become involved. But Caleb made the announcement that whoever wanted to marry Achsah would first have to kill some giants and take their land (see Joshua 15:16). This may have seemed to be an impossible challenge, but during that time there were giants living in the land. Caleb had killed a few of them, and he wanted to be sure that his daughter's husband could protect her from every type of enemy.

By requiring that his son-in-law be a giant killer, Caleb assured Achsah that her husband would not be lazy—lazy men do not fight giants. Also, she would be assured that her husband would be absolutely wild about her—only the man who sincerely loved her would be willing to risk his life to marry her.

Achsah probably wished her father hadn't issued that challenge. I am certain that her chances of finding a husband who would kill a giant looked very slim. But then *Othniel*, whose name means "force of God," showed up; and he certainly lived up to his name.

You see, Caleb was blessed by God and by men. He wisely blessed the future circumstances of Achsah's life by making it impossible for just anyone to marry her. I cannot emphasize this enough; parents need to bless their children—in every way. We also need to bless our children's future mates, before they ever meet.

The last example I want to give you about blessing each other's circumstances is Ruth, a Moabitess. Remember, the Moabites were cursed because of the incestuous relationship between Lot and his daughter, and sexual sin carries a terrible curse (see Deuteronomy 27:20-23).

Ruth also had been brought up in idolatry. The Moabites worshiped an idol called *Chemosh*, which means "a dung-hill deity." Idolatry also carries a curse—so Ruth was in double trouble! But both of those curses were absolutely reversed when Ruth turned to God. When she renounced Chemosh, the curses were broken totally and tremendous blessings came upon Ruth.

After Ruth's husband died, she decided to return to Bethlehem with Naomi instead of staying in Moab with her own family. She said to Naomi: "...Intreat me not to leave thee, or to return from following after thee: for whither thou goest, I will go; and where thou lodgest, I will lodge: thy people shall be my people, and thy God my God" (Ruth 1:16).

When they arrived in Bethlehem, Ruth went to work gleaning in the field of Naomi's wealthy relative Boaz. She followed Naomi's advice, and very soon Boaz wanted to marry Ruth. He went to the elders of the city and went through the tedious legal procedures involved with marrying Ruth (see Ruth 4). There were a lot of legalities that had to be worked out regarding property and children; but Boaz finally got everything straightened out, and he and Ruth were married.

Look at the blessings that the elders spoke into Boaz and Ruth's marriage:

...The LORD make the woman that is come into thine house like Rachel and like Leah, which two did build the house of Israel.... And let thy house be like the house of Pharez, whom Tamar bare unto Judah, of the seed which the LORD shall give thee of this woman.

Ruth 4:11,12

This ceremony was not only about a man taking a wife. More importantly, the elders also were blessing the circumstances of Boaz and Ruth's life together. The elders prayed for Ruth to be like Rachel and Leah, Jacob's wives who had borne the children who became the heads of the twelve tribes of Israel. The elders also prayed for Ruth to be like Judah's daughter-in-law

Tamar, who had borne twin sons, Pharez and Zarah (see Genesis 38:11-30). The children of these three women were blessed, and the elders were speaking the same blessings upon Ruth. But could Ruth's offspring be such a blessing? After all Rachel, Leah, and Tamar were Israelites while Ruth was a Moabitess.

You see, the Israelites knew the prophecy recorded in Genesis 3:15:

And I will put enmity between thee and the woman, and between thy seed and her seed; it shall bruise thy head, and thou shalt bruise his heel.

This is a Messianic prophecy, and all the Israelite women wanted to bring forth that seed. However, the Messiah would come only through the lineage of Judah: "The sceptre shall not depart from Judah, nor a lawgiver from between his feet, until Shiloh come; and unto him shall the gathering of the people be" (Genesis 49:10).

The Bible records five women in the genealogy of Jesus Christ, and Ruth is among these women (see Matthew 1:5). Do you wonder how she got there? Well, Boaz was from the tribe of Judah; and he and Ruth had a son named Obed. Obed's son was Jesse, and Jesse was the father of David. Ruth was David's grandmother; so she wound up in the genealogy of Jesus Christ!

God's blessings absolutely are powerful, and I pray that you will become a Satan-proofer and begin to function as a priest to the people closest to you. As you speak forth God's wonderful blessings, people will come into an attitude of worship and begin to walk in the tremendous benefits that accompany the manifestation of God's glory!

CHAPTER 7

—————⟫•⟪—————

Step On the Devil's Toes

What is a miracle? The dictionary defines a miracle as "an effect or extraordinary event in the physical world that surpasses all known human or natural powers and is ascribed to a supernatural cause." Miracles usually cause quite a stir in the lives of unbelievers—they have such a difficult time accepting that there is an almighty God who sometimes upsets the natural order of things and performs miracles.

But we, in the Body of Christ, know that when our heavenly Father performs a miracle—something beyond human or natural powers—He simply is making His presence known in the world. Therefore, believers should accept miracles as a normal part of our existence. In this chapter I'm going to show you how you can experience God's miracle-working power when you begin to sow miracles into the lives of others because when you sow you not only bless others, but you reap a miracle harvest as well.

Sometimes I wonder why so few Christians experience the marvelous, miracle-working power of God in their lives. Walking in the miraculous should be a normal everyday activity for Christians. Contrary to what many believers may think, miracles are not limited to the lives of people they believe to be "super Christians." Miracles occur in the lives of ordinary believers, like you and me, who have been empowered by an extraordinary God to accomplish supernatural things.

When you received Christ as your Savior, you literally became a miracle. By the power of God, you entered into a new realm—a supernatural realm where the impossible becomes possible because of faith. What faith? Your faith in Jesus Christ that allows you to stand on and to live according to every Word that comes forth from the mouth of God.

"But ye shall receive power, after that the Holy Ghost is come upon you...."

Acts 1:8

God's Word says that believers will receive power. The Greek word here for power is *dunamis,* which means miraculous power, ability, strength, violence, and abundance.[1] We get our word *dynamite* from the word *dunamis.* God's dunamis—His miracle-working power—operating in your life will give you the ability to rise up strong in the Holy Spirit. You will become an explosive force in the spiritual realm.

If you are a Spirit-filled believer, then God's miracle-working power is within you. As a Satan-proofer you are the recipient of an "extraordinary-ness" that surpasses all known human or natural powers—the Holy Spirit.

There is another word for power that I want to look at:

Behold, I give unto you power to tread on serpents and scorpions, and over all the power of the enemy: and nothing shall by any means hurt you.

Luke 10:19

In this scripture, the power of the enemy is miracle-working power. The Bible gives many examples of demonic miracles being performed, beginning when the serpent spoke with Eve:

...And he [the serpent] *said unto the woman, Yea, hath God said, Ye shall not eat of every tree of the garden?*

Genesis 3:1

Can you imagine yourself having a conversation with a snake? That certainly would qualify as an extraordinary event that surpassed all known human powers—a miracle. What about when Moses went before Pharaoh? The Egyptian sorcerers performed almost exactly the same miracles as did Moses— their rods became serpents, they caused the waters in the Nile River to turn to blood, and they caused frogs to come forth in a plague. (See Exodus 7:12,22; 8:7.) These events, although extraordinary happenings, definitely were not caused by God.

Now look back at Luke 10:19 where it says power to tread on serpents and scorpions. Here the Greek word used for power is *exousia*, which means "authority."[2]

Satan's miracle-working power absolutely pales when compared to the authority of God. God has given authority and miracle-working power to believers—to step all over the devil! And there is no question that when you begin to sow miracles into the lives of others, you are going to have to step on the devil's toes.

You received God's authority the moment you were born again; and if you have been baptized in the Holy Spirit, you have been given God's miracle-working power. So when you think of becoming a Satan-proofer by sowing miracles into the lives of other, I want you to know that God absolutely has equipped you to handle this challenge; and through Christ Jesus, you can do it!

Operating in the Extraordinary

As I said earlier, Christians should be involved in the miraculous as a normal occurrence. What stops us? I believe God's power operating in our lives is hindered when we become tangled up in our old nature. For various reasons, we sometimes harbor negative thoughts, attitudes, or emotions like unforgiveness, bitterness, anger, or resentment. These things are products of our old nature; and believe me, they will stop God's miracle-working power from flowing freely in our lives.

I want to talk to you about your emotions. Sometimes it is so easy to become negative. My heart almost breaks when I hear about the terrible suffering that some believers have experienced at the hands of others. If you are one of them, you have reason to be angry and hurt—these are normal emotional responses. But did you know that your emotions provide one of Satan's favorite playgrounds? An emotional response to a situation may be normal, but Satan can invade your emotions. Before you know it, that normal response may turn into a sinful condition:

> *Be angry, and sin not: ...Neither give place to the devil.*
>
> Ephesians 4:26-27

If you want to sow miracles into the lives of others, then you will need to Satan-proof your emotions. God knows that sometimes you may become angry; but if you allow Satan to inflate your emotions, your anger may turn into hate. There are times when you may experience disappointment. If you aren't careful, Satan can intensify your feelings and you may become severely depressed and discouraged.

But remember, all these negative things are part of our old nature, and we cannot experience God's miracle-working power in that condition. God wants us all to be Satan-proofers and to overcome our old nature so we can operate in our new nature on a consistent basis. That's when believers really begin to walk in the miraculous. I want to tell you about a bona fide Satan-proofer who literally sowed miracles into her enemy's life.

Years ago a woman in our city came to me and shared how her daughter—a Bible-school student in her thirties—had been stabbed to death! What a horrible tragedy! The mother told me how she had gone into a deep depression as a result of her overwhelming grief. She soon became bitter toward God and built up a tremendous hatred for the murderer, who, after taking the lives of many more women, had finally been apprehended.

One Saturday night God spoke to my friend and said, "If you don't forgive that murderer, I cannot forgive you because if you don't forgive the trespasses of others, I can't forgive you of yours." Maybe she felt she had a right to be angry and hurt, but God insisted that she forgive the man.

So this dear lady reached out to God; and by faith, she forgave her daughter's murderer. The next day God gave her an opportunity to act out her faith;

and in doing so, she sowed a miracle into the man's life. The Gideons came to her church, and she made a contribution for Bibles. Then she asked one of the Gideons to go and present a Bible personally to her daughter's murderer, who was in prison.

Yes, you know what happened. God performed a miracle in that vicious killer's heart, and he became a victorious Christian. He literally became a missionary in that prison!

The woman sowed another miracle into this man's life and paid for his correspondence Bible school material. One day she said to me, "Marilyn, the devil murdered my daughter, who was going to be a missionary; but God, in His great mercy, took my daughter's murderer and made him a missionary in a place where my daughter could never go!" Friend, *this is a miracle!*

In your new nature, you will sow blessings and miracles even into the lives of your enemies.

How did it happen? This woman certainly had the right to be angry and hurt. That man had brutally murdered her daughter! Whether knowingly or unknowingly, he had allowed himself to be used by the devil and had harmed many people. But did my friend allow Satan to turn her anger into hate? *No!* She sowed a miracle into this man's life and reaped a tremendous miracle in her own—the peace that passes all understanding over her daughter's death. That was extraordinary and certainly surpassed all human powers!

My friend took authority over any evil effort that the devil wanted to exert in her emotions. By faith she stepped out of the realm of her emotions and into the realm of the supernatural—the miraculous! By doing so, she became a conduit for God's authority and miracle-working power to flow into the murderer's life. These miracles probably wouldn't have occurred if the woman had been operating according to her emotions. She sowed a miracle, and miracles continue to multiply each time another prisoner gets saved.

We all need to Satan-proof our emotions. Friend, let me say that one of the many roadblocks the devil will use to hinder you from receiving God's miracles is to keep you operating in your emotions—your old nature. However, through Christ Jesus, you have been given God's authority to step out of the realm of your emotions into the realm of the supernatural—your new nature.

In your new nature, you will sow blessings and miracles even into the lives of your enemies. After all, in terms of people, your enemies are just victims (as we saw in an earlier chapter), who, either knowingly or unknowingly, have allowed the devil to manipulate them into hurting you. When you begin to bless and sow miracles in the lives of these people, then you will begin to walk in the miraculous on a more consistent basis in your own life.

You may say, "Scripture says I have authority to tread on serpents and scorpions. I thought that meant the devil, not my emotions." You're right! But the devil can magnify your emotions to a very negative level; and if you aren't careful, your emotions can easily get out of control and you'll end up in a sinful condition.

My friend could have allowed the devil to invade her emotions and turn the normal grieving process into bitterness. There isn't a more deadly sting than the results of a life lived in anger. And just as the poison from a snake (serpent) can destroy you, so can bitterness and anger destroy your relationships, your hopes, and your dreams.

Let me encourage you if you have had a painful experience with another person: You must begin to Satan-proof your emotions, keeping in mind that your heavenly Father is El Shaddai, "the Lord who is more than enough." His Holy Spirit in you makes you more than enough to overcome any negative feelings or thoughts that you may be harboring against someone. You will no longer focus on the terrible thing that may have been done to you. Instead, you'll focus on Jesus Christ; and you'll begin to operate in your new nature. Christ in you will take you out of the ordinary into the extraordinary, and you'll respond to your adversaries with love. It's your attitude toward people that determines your altitude in the miracle-working power of God.

I believe we have probably all had occasions where a person has verbally, emotionally, or physically abused us. And if something bad happens to the person, we may think, "Goody, goody! That's what they deserve." You may have felt that way at one time or another; sometimes I have too. But that's really an ugly attitude, straight out of our old nature:

> *Rejoice not when thine enemy falleth, and let not thine heart be glad when he stumbleth. Lest the LORD see it, and it displease him....*

> Proverbs 24:17-18

This verse does not refer to our real enemy, the devil, but to people who harm us. Regardless what the circumstances may be, God says, "I know how you feel; but don't rejoice in another's catastrophes, it will displease Me."

The Bible is quite clear when it talks about how we are to treat our enemies. Jesus said: "But I say unto you, Love your enemies, bless them that curse you, do good to them that hate you, and pray for them which despitefully use you and persecute you" (Matthew 5:44). We are to love them, bless them, pray for them, and do good for them—we are to sow miracles into the lives of our enemies. Now, your old nature doesn't want to do these things; but your new nature, the one you received when you were born again, wants to do good for all people.

God wants to set you free from wrong thinking and wrong attitudes that come out of your old nature. God wants you to become a Satan-proofer and get out of the realm of your emotions so you can reach into the supernatural and pull down miracles for your life and for others as well.

Step Into Your Faith Nature

You may be thinking right now, *I just can't control my emotions.* But that simply is not true because, in Christ, you can do all things (see Philippians 4:13). The Bible contains many examples of believers who chose to serve God rather than their emotions—they are not all big names like Jesus, Elijah, Moses, or Paul either. Some of their names are not even mentioned—for instance, Naaman's wife's handmaiden.

At one time in Israel's history, Syria had repeatedly come down and attacked God's people. One of the major leaders in the Syrian army was a man named Naaman (see 2 Kings 5:1). On one of his campaigns against Israel, the Syrians had taken captive a little Jewish girl who had become a servant to his wife.

Imagine the emotional tearing this young girl must have experienced being kidnapped from her home and forced into slavery by the Syrians. Then one day she learned that her mistress' husband had the dreaded disease leprosy. It must have been difficult for her to resist the urge to rejoice at Naaman's calamity and say, "He stole me from my parents, my temple, and my life. He deserves to have leprosy because he killed a lot of my relatives!" But she didn't rejoice; instead, she said to her mistress: "...Would God my lord were with the prophet that is in Samaria; for he would recover him of his leprosy" (2 Kings 5:3).

I want to compare Namaan's servant's response with the response of a woman who was forced to endure a different kind of slavery. One of my Bible school students shared that from the age of seven to the age of sixteen, she had been sexually abused by her stepmother's brother. Many times she went to her parents and told them how she had been enslaved to this man's sickening behavior, but they didn't believe her. Inevitably, she became pregnant; and through some very painful circumstances, she miscarried her child.

I praise God that this young woman eventually got out of that abusive environment, and now she is born again and Spirit-filled. She has done missionary work in Africa, Japan, Korea, and the Virgin Islands; and she has a tremendous desire to become involved in a prayer ministry. It took time, but God has healed her emotionally and physically from the damage inflicted upon her while she was growing up.

However, one day her step-uncle injured himself when he fell from a ladder; and the doctors said he would never walk again. Now watch how God performed a miracle in this situation. If the young woman had allowed herself to operate from her old nature, she could have really rejoiced at the calamity of the man who had destroyed her precious childhood. Instead, she sowed a miracle into his life, and she forgave her abuser! Then she led him to the Lord! Now he, his wife, and most of their children are saved and serving God!

Quite honestly, most of us want to see God's miracles occurring in our own lives, but we rarely want to sow miracles into the lives of other people—especially the lives of our enemies. But let me tell you, sowing and reaping and asking for miracles go together like Siamese twins.

Look at what happened when Naaman's little Jewish servant resisted the urge to "snicker and gloat" over Naaman's mishap. She sowed a miracle into Naaman's life by suggesting that he go and see the prophet Elisha. Naaman visited Elisha and was miraculously healed of leprosy. But he wasn't just healed of the disease; the greater miracle occurred in Naaman's heart:

And he returned to the man of God, he and all his company, and came, and stood before him: and he said, Behold, now I know that there is no God in all the earth, but in Israel....

2 Kings 5:15

Naaman is never mentioned again as one who led an attack against Israel. Why? Because his life was changed, and he no longer was Israel's enemy:

When a man's ways please the Lord, he maketh even his enemies to be at peace with him.

Proverbs 16:7

Naaman probably went back to Syria and presented himself before his king and gave a tremendous testimony! But the Syrian king didn't seem to be impressed by the miracle-working power of the God of Israel.

You know, sometimes we believers get into a similar mind set. We can see God's wonderful miracle-working power in action in someone else's life but refuse to accept miracles in our own lives. One man in our church found it difficult to believe that divine healing flowed so easily through our congregation. He didn't believe that people could be in severe pain one moment and be completely pain free the next.

Then he injured his leg. When he came to church, his leg was swollen, blue, and throbbing with pain. The Holy Spirit led us into a healing service, and you guessed it—our friend who was in severe pain one moment was completely pain free the next.

Nevertheless, God's miracle-working power didn't affect the Syrian king. He continued to attack Israel again and again. However, his armies never succeeded in surprising the Israelites—they always seemed to know when and where their enemy was going to attack. It would have been natural for the Syrian king to assume there was a traitor in his camp. He demanded to know, "Who is the dirty traitor":

And one of his servants said, None, my lord, O king: but Elisha, the prophet that is in Israel, telleth the king of Israel the words that thou speakest in thy bedchamber.

2 Kings 6:12

Elisha certainly was a tremendous man of faith. By faith Elisha heard the king making secret plans to attack Israel—in the privacy of the royal bedroom! The Bible says: "The secret things belong unto the LORD our God: but those things which are revealed belong unto us . . ." (Deuteronomy 29:29).

Because God knows the secret plots of men, He can lead us by His Spirit so we won't fall into the enemy's snares. I think sometimes we Christians believe that if we don't bang our enemies around, our enemies will bang us around. But I am going to tell you that if you stay true to God, He will show you the secrets of your enemies and protect you from them. And what does God want you to do with what He reveals to you about your enemies? He wants you to bless them, to pray for them, and to sow miracles into their lives. All of this comes out of our new nature—our faith nature.

I received a letter from a woman in Dallas who wrote of how God dealt with her about being involved in an adult book store business. She terminated her involvement and then challenged her husband to do the same. He refused and chose to stay involved in pornography rather than to continue with his marriage to this courageous Christian lady. She said in her letter:

> *While my husband and I were separated, he became acquainted with a girl who was a hooker and a cocaine addict. At first I was angry, bitter, and really hurt. My prayers seemed to go unanswered.*

Then one day:

> *A voice spoke to me saying, Read about forgiveness.... I prayed a prayer and spoke my husband's name first and then the girl's name, forgiving them both. The peace and love and joy I found and felt at that moment couldn't be described. It was truly the peace that passes all understanding. After that prayer, God began to open my eyes and heart for this girl. For 13 months I prayed for her, eating, sleeping, and breathing for her salvation.*

Eventually the woman's marriage was restored, and the "other woman" ended up in prison. While she was imprisoned, this woman received Christ as her Savior and began witnessing to the guards and inmates!

Do you see what happened here? She was betrayed by her husband and injured by this other woman. She allowed the devil to invade the normal emotional reaction and escalate it into bitterness and resentment, which was in her old nature. The minute that she got into her old nature, her prayers went unanswered. Friend, as long as you are in your old nature, you will not experience God's miracle-working power in your life.

When this lady stepped out of the realm of her emotions and into the realm of the supernatural, God intervened in her situation and brought about a change. Was it an easy thing for her to accomplish? No, but in her new nature—the Christlike nature— loving her enemy became possible.

Elisha was operating in the supernatural realm—the faith realm.

Get a Double Miracle

When you begin to sow miracles into the lives of your "enemies," don't be surprised when the devil really zeroes in on you. That Syrian king told his servants to find Elisha, "...Go and spy where he is, that I may send and fetch him. And it was told him saying, Behold, he is in Dothan" (2 Kings 6:13). Elisha was in the city of Dothan, which means "a double decree." When you sow miracles into the lives of other people, you'll get a double miracle—one in their lives and one in your life too.

I am always amazed that the Syrian king felt it necessary to send so many soldiers to capture Elisha: "Therefore sent he thither horses, and chariots, and a great host: and they came by night, and compassed the city about" (2 Kings 6:14).

All these soldiers were trying to sneak up on Elisha in the middle of the night, but remember that God was revealing their plans to Elisha. Although he knew they were coming, do you think Elisha was nervous? No way! Elisha was operating in the supernatural realm—the faith realm. Now his servant was the one who had the problem. He was absolutely terrified.

Look at how lovingly Elisha dealt with his servant. Elisha didn't jump down his throat saying, "You're not supposed to be afraid. Haven't you been listening to what I have been teaching you?" Rather, Elisha sowed a miracle into his servant's life:

And Elisha prayed, and said, LORD, I pray thee, open his eyes, that he may see. And the LORD opened the eyes of the young man; and he saw: and, behold, the mountain was full of horses and chariots of fire round about Elisha.

2 Kings 6:17

Elisha prayed for a miracle, and prayer is the major means by which you are going to see God's miracle-working power flow into your life too. Elijah sowed a miracle through prayer, and this young servant saw the divine protection that God has for His people.

When the servant looked up, he saw that the mountain was full of horses and chariots of fire! Certainly he recalled Elisha's testimony about how Elijah had been taken up in a chariot of fire. Now he was seeing firsthand that God's chariots of fire were there for Elisha too. Did you notice that Elisha didn't pray for himself to see God's divine protection? Elisha operated in a supernatural realm, and by faith he knew God's miracle-working power would work in his circumstances just as it had worked in Elijah's.

So many times when we are facing new challenges, we need to keep in mind that the same God who delivered us in the past certainly is able to deliver us in the present. Even though we may not always be able to see the end results, we can be certain that God's protection is around His people. The Bible asks a very profound question:

...If God be for us, who can be against us?

Romans 8:31

The answer, of course, is *no one*! There will always be more standing for God's people than against them. Look at Elisha; the Syrians had surrounded his house. Can you imagine a whole army coming to get one little man? I think that is almost funny. The king of Syria obviously was afraid of Elisha.

Did you know that the devil is afraid of you? One little Christian frightens Satan silly. He knows that when you begin to operate in your new nature—your faith nature and begin to walk out into the authority and the miracle-working power of God—then he has had it!

94

Elisha prayed for another miracle:

…Smite this people I pray thee, with blindness. And he smote them with blindness according to the word of Elisha.

2 Kings 6:18

Isn't it interesting that God opened the eyes of Elisha's servant, and then closed the eyes of Elisha's enemies? I think there have been times when God has closed the eyes of officials when my ministry team has taken the Word of God into communist countries.

One time we were taking Bibles into Poland. We also wanted to make a video, so we had 13 pieces of video equipment with us. We had been warned that the customs officers might confiscate our equipment when we got to Warsaw because the government didn't like the idea of Christians coming into their country making videos. However, we believed God was leading us; so we prayed before we got off the plane, "Lord, help us to come through and get all our videos in and out quickly and safely—even if You have to blind the eyes of the customs people."

The customs officer was a woman. She had an ugly attitude and really gave me a hard time. But when she saw my associate who had the 13 pieces of video equipment, she smiled so sweetly at him and told him to go through. I don't believe she even saw the equipment. I believe God closed her eyes to the equipment that we needed to perform what He had called us to do in Poland.

Similarly, God had blinded the Syrian soldiers; then Elisha tricked them into going to Samaria the capital of Israel. When they arrived, Israel's king Jehoram said to Elisha: "…My father, shall I smite them? shall I smite them?" (2 Kings 6:21).

Jehoram probably thought, *What an opportunity to kill all these Syrians. They are just like sitting ducks!*

That was a natural response, but God's Word tells us to love our enemies. We are to pray for them, to bless them, and to do good to them. And don't forget, it was God's miracle-working power that had brought the enemy to the king's front door in the first place. Why did God do it? To show forth His marvelous mercy. You see the Lord is not only a Friend to believers; He is also a

Friend to sinners. God has destined that all people would come to repentance so we all can be born again and Spirit-filled.

When Jehoram exposed his desire to kill the Syrians, Elisha answered: "...Thou shalt not smite them: wouldest thou smite those whom thou halt taken captive with thy sword and with thy bow? set bread and water before them, that they may eat and drink, and go to their master" (2 Kings 6:22).

Doesn't God's Word tell us that if our enemy is hungry, we are to feed him, to give him water if he is thirsty? If you can pray for your enemies and sow miracles into their lives, that in itself is a miracle. It means that you are a Satan-proofer doing extraordinary things that surpass human power. You'll be operating out of your new nature; and through Jesus Christ, you will accomplish the miraculous.

You know, if you are looking for a double feast of God's miracle-working power in your life, you must come out of your old nature. Elisha could have led those blind men right over the edge of a cliff; or he could have said to Jehoram, "Yes! Go ahead and kill them." That certainly would have been the natural thing to do. However, Elisha was not operating in the natural; he was operating in the supernatural; and he showed forth God's marvelous mercies to Israel's enemies. They fed the Syrian army and sent them home.

That certainly must have been a huge grocery bill. But it always costs you something when you choose to walk in the miraculous and sow love, peace, joy, and righteousness into the lives of others.

Sowing the Firstfruits

When you see the word "firstfruits" in the Bible, it identifies God's priorities. Needless to say, God's firstfruits—priorities—may not always be ours (even though they should be). What are God's firstfruits? God is just wild over people! We are His number-one priority. The Bible says, "And God blessed them, and God said unto them, Be fruitful and multiply, and replenish the earth...." (Genesis 1:28).

This Scripture lets us know that God loved people so much that He was not satisfied with just one couple; He wanted the earth to be inhabited with lots and lots of people. So He told Adam and Eve, "I want you to go forth and bring forth fruit—have children—and replenish the earth." Notice how God refers to people as "fruit." I guess we could say that God's favorite fruit is children: "Lo, children are an heritage of the LORD: and the fruit of the womb is his reward" (Psalms 127:3).

Later, God told the Israelites that their firstfruits—their firstborn male children—belonged to Him. However, instead of literally taking their babies away from them, God designated the entire tribe of Levites to symbolize the firstfruits of the nation of Israel:

> *And thou shalt take the Levites for me (I am the Lord) instead of all the firstborn among the children of Israel....*

> Numbers 3:41

The Israelites participated in a dedication ceremony for their children, and on the thirtieth day after the first male child was born, the mother and the father presented their baby to the priest. The priest would ask the mother, "Is this your firstborn son?" She would say, "Yes, it is." Then the priest would ask the father, "Is this your firstborn son?" and the father would respond, "Yes, it is." By affirming the child to be their firstborn, these parents symbolically gave the child to God.

Then the parents were required to redeem their child—buy him back—by paying the priest five shekels (about $3.20). (See Numbers 3:40-50.) You may think it pretty strange that they had to buy back their own child—and for only $3.20! Actually this was a tax that God had imposed to help support the priests and Levites.

However, the concept of redemption is extremely important to you and me today because believers have been redeemed (see Galatians 3:13). We have not been redeemed with corruptible things like silver and gold, but with the precious blood of Jesus (see 1 Peter 1:18; Revelation 5:9). Since God has destined for all people to come into His family, every person born on this earth is a potential firstborn child of God. Do you see how people are God's number-one priority?

People aren't God's only firstfruits. God also talked to the Israelites about the firstfruits of their harvest (see Exodus 23:16). God said, "Make Me your priority. Put Me first in whatever you do. At the beginning of the harvest, bring Me your firstfruits." Today, you give God the firstfruits of your harvests when you pay your tithes—ten percent of your pretax income—to the storehouse (your local church). You are saying, "God, You are the priority in my life. You are my source, and I am returning my firstfruits to You."

I received a testimony from a man who said he had been delivered from debt and decrease. He had been employed with an oil company; and although his annual income was just under $50,000, he acquired a $340,000 debt! Then he went through a divorce, changed jobs, and ended up making less than $24,000 per year. Needless to say, he could not pay off the large amount of money he owed.

But something else happened to him that year. He rededicated his life to the Lord, became Spirit-filled, and began to learn about tithing. His letter said, "I am absolutely convinced that if you do not tithe, the devourer is not going to be rebuked. However, if you do tithe, I don't care how big your bills are …what God does is to give you favor with your creditors, and that's something I've learned to claim."

This man didn't know how God was going to set him free of financial bondage, but he was determined to tithe despite how futile his financial situation appeared.

Then he said that God began to speak to his heart about giving offerings of $150 to $ 500 above his normal tithe. At one point, he began to question whether or not he really was hearing from God; he wondered if his mind was playing tricks on him. However, each time He obeyed God in the area of giving, God would supernaturally bless him.

By the next year, his debt had been reduced to $250,000 and God said, "I'm going to heal your finances." This man is seeing evidence of this promise more and more each day.

God has commanded His people to tithe, "Bring ye all the tithes into the storehouse…" (Malachi 3:10). It's too bad that many Christians allow God to deliver them from all sorts of sinful lifestyles—they attend church regularly and they study their Bibles—but they are not committed tithers. Then they wonder why they never seem to be able to accomplish their financial goals. It's because they do not trust God to Satan-proof their finances by tithing their firstfruits:

And I will rebuke the devourer for your sakes, and he shall not destroy the fruits of your ground....

Malachi 3:11

I have noticed that people who faithfully pay their tithes seem to have much more than people who don't. I have heard some amazing testimonies of how God has taken 90 percent of someone's income and stretched it to meet all financial needs, with some left over. When Christians share their financial problems with me, I always ask, "Do you tithe?" Some people respond, "No, I can't afford it." I tell them, "You really can't afford not to tithe."

The truth is, whether we like it or not, we have to obey God; and He said that our tithes—firstfruits—belong to Him. When we give God our firstfruits, it's as if we are planting a seed. God will multiply that seed and bring forth a great harvest.

> *I have noticed that people who faithfully pay their tithes seem to have much more than people who don't.*

Another one of God's firstfruits is the nation of Israel, "Israel was holiness unto the Lord, and the firstfruits of his increase: all that devour him shall offend; evil shall come upon them, saith the Lord" (Jeremiah 2:3).

God claimed the whole nation of Israel as His; and whenever God talks about His "firsts," He is planning on a big harvest. So, although Israel may have been God's first nation, look at the millions of people from other nations who became born again because of God's dealings with the Israelites.

Israel was the seed from which God expected a great harvest of many other nations to become His people. The same principle will work for us today concerning our loved ones. For example, when we dedicate our children to God as infants and bring them up in the fear and admonition of God, what happens? God becomes their priority, and they will begin to witness to others about the love of Jesus Christ. They will begin to turn on God's light in people's lives, and this will cause others to come to Christ.

Have you ever heard people say, "You can't outgive God?" That certainly is true; and we can see this when God said, "Because people are my priority and I am asking them to give to Me their firstfruits, I am going to give back to them My best—My firstborn Son." Who is God's firstborn Son? Yes, it's Jesus.

For whom he did foreknow, he also did predestinate to be conformed to the image of his Son, that he might be the firstborn among many brethren.

Romans 8:29

In whom we have redemption through his blood, even the forgiveness of sins: Who is the image of the invisible God, the firstborn of every creature.

Colossians 1:14,15

And again, when he bringeth in the firstbegotten into the world, he saith, And let all the angels of God worship him.

Hebrews 1:6

God gave us His firstborn, Jesus, because He wanted a harvest—a great big family of firstborns. He wanted us all to come into His kingdom and be firstborns too. God's number-one priority is people. We have always been God's first concern.

Worth the Cost

Earlier we saw that all people are destined—set apart—to subdue the earth and to be blessed—to be put in an attitude of worship. This can only take place after our minds have been renewed, and we have been conformed into the image of Jesus Christ. Right? Therefore, it's when we become born again that we become God's firstborn.

I really want you to understand that you must be born again. Just because your parents may be born-again Christians does not automatically mean that you are a Christian. No, you have to receive Christ into your life. Your parents may stand in faith for your salvation, but you personally have to be born again.

When you become born again, you become a firstborn because Jesus is God's firstborn—you come into God's family through your faith in Christ. Now look at what Jesus says about you:

And I have declared unto them thy name, and will declare it: that the love wherewith thou hast, loved me may be in them, and I in them.

John 17:26

Jesus said that His heavenly Father loves you just as much as He loves Jesus. I know it may sound too wonderful to be true; nonetheless, God loves you just as much as He loves His firstborn—Jesus.

Salvation is free, but serving the Lord will cost you something. Do you know what it costs? It costs you your old nature, which really isn't a terribly big price to pay in order to see God's wonderful miracles occurring in your life on a more consistent basis.

CHAPTER 8

Securing Your Future

I really get inspired when I read the book of Hebrews. Chapter 11 is sometimes referred to as the "Hall of Fame" for our biblical faith heroes. It absolutely overflows with examples of ordinary people who walked in godly wisdom. They put their faith in an extraordinary God and supernaturally Satan-proofed their future.

Through the lives of Abraham, Isaac, Jacob, and Joseph, we are going to see how we can walk in godly wisdom and, by faith, secure our future. You may say, "Marilyn, I want to do that, and I want to secure my loved ones' future too, but I don't know how to get godly wisdom." The Bible tells you how:

If any of you lack wisdom, let him ask of God, that giveth to all men liberally, and upbraideth not; and it shall be given to him.

James 1:5

The Greek word used here for *wisdom* means "a clarity in spiritual things." In order to secure your future, you need to get a better understanding of the things of God. You need to know how to secure your future according to God's plan for your life. In order to know what God has planned for you and your loved ones, you'll have to seek Him.

We live in a time of uncertainty—in our personal lives as well as in the world. Some people live in a constant state of fear because they focus on the statistics on crime, abortion, and substance abuse, which continue to increase at an alarming rate. Many times they have experienced firsthand the heartbreaking results of the demise of God's first established institution—marriage. People look at all the unrest in the world, and they desperately wonder, *Oh dear, what's going on? Things are getting worse and worse; what will become of us?*

Praise God! Why? Because in the midst of all this chaos, you the believer, don't have to worry! You are a covenant child of El Elyon, the Most High[1] God; you can have the highest confidence because God has big plans for your future. However, you're going to have to begin walking in faith and in God's wisdom if you want to see His plans manifested in your future.

There are three blessings that we can look at when we talk about securing our future: material, inheritance, and victory. Despite the circumstances around you, God wants you to know that you, His child, have been blessed. When you live your life in an attitude of worship, you put yourself in a position to inherit everything that God has destined for you—eternal life, to be baptized into the Holy Spirit, and to be conformed into the wonderful image of Jesus Christ. In the image of Christ, you'll subdue the earth (your environment) and bear the fruit that accompanies victorious life (good health, financial security, and peace of mind).

You may think, *Well, I'm born again. I love the Lord; but my health is bad, my finances are a mess, and my nerves are just about shot!* Do you wonder why you don't seem to be able to get it together and to walk in prosperity like other Christians? Be encouraged because, although that may be where you are today, I believe that when you begin to walk in faith and godly wisdom, your life, health, and finances are going to do a complete turnaround. Your future will be secured according to God's desires for your life, and His plans for you to be victorious over your circumstances.

Step Out in Godly Wisdom

As you begin to focus more intently on God's will for you and your loved ones and begin more seriously to seek God through prayer, Bible study, and application of God's Word, then you'll start to become a Satan-proofer. And there absolutely is no question, your life will change and your future will be secured in God's Word.

Again, the key to a secured future is walking in godly wisdom. Let's get very practical. What do you do after you have prayed and asked God for wisdom? You spend a lot of time with God, and He will show you exactly how to apply the Scriptures to your circumstances. That's how you begin to secure your future by faith and godly wisdom.

By faith Isaac blessed Jacob and Esau ...Jacob, ...blessed both the sons of Joseph; ...Joseph, ...made mention of the departing of the children of Israel; and gave commandment concerning his bones.

Hebrews 11:20-22

All these men secured their future by faith! Where did they put their faith? In God. And when they began to step out in His Word and His wisdom, they secured the future for themselves and for their loved ones.

I believe Abraham had a pretty clear understanding of spiritual things. When he walked in godly wisdom, Abraham secured the future for himself, his descendants, and, actually, the world. Abraham is sometimes called the "father of faith," and there is no question that he was a man of supernatural faith. But even though he had faith, Abraham did not always walk in godly wisdom; and the results were disastrous.

Abraham acted in great faith when he first encountered God; and God instructed Abraham to leave his home in Haran and to travel to an unknown destination. Can you imagine the conversation that may have occurred between Abraham and Sarah that night?

"Sarah, God told me to leave Haran."

"All right, Abraham, but where are we going?"

"Oh, I don't know; God didn't say. But He did say that in me would all the families of the earth be blessed." (See Genesis 12:1-3.) "So Abram departed, as the LORD had spoken unto him; ...Abram was seventy and five years old when he departed out of Haran" (v. 4).

When you think about this 75-year-old man and his household, you may be picturing some little band of nomads trudging off through the countryside. But actually Abraham had a huge household. He had many slaves, among them at least 318 trained soldiers and their wives and families (see Genesis 14:14). And this doesn't count Lot's household! So when Abraham packed up his household and left Haran, he may have been leading a caravan of several thousand people.

At this point, I'm not sure how much godly wisdom Abraham walked in; but he certainly was wise enough to recognize and to obey God's instructions.

I love to hear the testimonies from my Bible school students and from the members of my staff. There are so many cases where God literally has called people to pack up and move to Denver. One of our pastors had called my husband and me to say he and his wife believed that God was calling them to Denver to become involved in our ministry. At that time there were no positions available, but they were convinced that Denver was in God's plan for their future.

So we all prayed about it. Not long after that, an opening became available which was just tailor-made for their capabilities. This couple walked in God's wisdom for their future, and they have been such a tremendous blessing to us.

Now I want you to know that you will always have a choice as to whether you are going to walk wisely in spiritual things or not. This couple could have rationalized God's instructions to them about moving; after all, they pastored a thriving church in California. Similarly, Abraham could have said, "Oh, I'm just not sure; maybe that wasn't God's voice. I'd better stay here in Haran."

But Abraham didn't say that. He had tremendous faith in God, which really was supernatural because he had been an idolater. He didn't have a Bible, there were no church services—no evangelist came to Abraham's city to get him saved— no, it was God's spoken Word that convicted Abraham. Abraham stepped out on the Word and, by faith, secured the future not only for himself, but also for all the people who depended upon him. Abraham served God, and he demanded that his entire household serve God along with him (see Genesis 18:19).

As I said earlier, Abraham was a man of great faith, but he didn't always walk in godly wisdom. There is a difference between walking in faith and walking in wisdom. One time after Abraham had been living in Canaan for about ten years, Sarah began to get nervous because she and Abraham hadn't conceived a child yet. She may have been thinking about God's promise that all the families on earth would be blessed through Abraham. How could that happen unless a child was born to Abraham?

Then Sarah got an idea that she thought would "speed up" God's timetable. Evidently the customs of the day allowed for an unusual way of conceiving an heir to whom one would leave their property. So Sarah cooked up a scheme whereby Abraham would become sexually involved with Hagar, her Egyptian servant, and the child from that union would be Abraham's heir.

When Abraham heard the idea, he could have said, "No Sarah, God did not tell me to do things that way. We are going to trust God's Word to instruct us in our plans for the future." However, we know that Abraham went along with Sarah's kooky idea; and he and Hagar produced a son named Ishmael. I believe that Abraham and Sarah probably thought they had secured their future; but actually they were not in faith—they were operating in flesh. Ishmael was not the promised seed; Isaac was.

Abraham did not walk in God's wisdom for that situation. He may have had great faith to leave his homeland and to follow God into parts unknown, but faith without wisdom can cause big trouble for a believer.

The Bible indicates that about ten years passed before God communicated with Abraham again (see Genesis 17:1). This time God appeared to Abraham and told him to walk before Him and to be perfect. In other words, "Abraham, do things My way; and be sincere and upright in your walk."

It is imperative that we Christians do things God's way if we want to Satan-proof our lives and secure our future. As long as Abraham did things his way, disaster followed; but when he began to walk in faith and godly wisdom for his circumstances, blessings followed.

Abraham and Sarah finally got onto the right track. Together they had a son Isaac; however, the tension continued to grow between Sarah and Hagar until Abraham was forced to expel Hagar and his firstborn son, Ishmael, from his household. Sometimes I feel so sorry for Hagar and Ishmael. But then I know that God is so wonderful, and He loves all people. When Hagar and

Ishmael began to cry out to God, He showed forth His marvelous mercies; and God secured their future with His provisions.

Laying Up Treasures in Heaven

Abraham and Sarah raised Isaac according to God's Word; and just before Abraham died, he blessed Isaac with his substance: "And Abraham gave all that he had unto Isaac" (Genesis 25:5).

It's interesting that, despite having other sons by his concubine and by his second wife, Keturah, Abraham gave all his wealth to Isaac. Abraham didn't ignore his other children—he gave them gifts; but he also sent them away from Isaac. Abraham's experience with Hagar and Ishmael probably taught him a lesson about strife—godly wisdom was employed to secure Isaac's future and to keep all his brothers from laying claim to Isaac's inheritance.

After Abraham died, God blessed Isaac and secured his future:

And it came to pass after the death of Abraham, that God blessed his son Isaac; and Isaac dwelt by the well Lahai-roi.

Genesis 25:11

The Hebrew definition of *Lahai-roi* means "a well of life." Isaac was really blessed, but who actually blessed his future? When Abraham was alive, he did all he could for his son; but God actually blessed Isaac's future. Abraham had sown the seeds—he prayed about Isaac and prepared his son to receive God's future plans. Although Abraham had claimed blessings for Isaac, it was God who really gave life to Isaac's future.

One morning I was praying out on our back porch. I remember it was so pretty that summer, and it just seemed as if the Lord had opened up the heavens to me while I was praying. He asked me, "Did you know that when you pray, you are laying up treasures in heaven?" I thought, *Well, Father, I know we say that about our giving, but I didn't know about prayers*. God went on to explain that when I prayed, it was as if I was depositing into a bank account. All the prayers I deposited would come down upon the people I had prayed for—blessings would come upon their lives as they drew out of my prayer account. I have seen some of the prayers come to pass; but, if Jesus tarries, some may not be manifested until after I die.

The prayers we pray in the present will bless people in the future. When believers are walking in godly wisdom, they have strong, consistent prayer lives. Prayer will bring you into a more intimate relationship with your heavenly Father, and God will share some wonderful revelations about how to apply His Word to your circumstances during those precious times of fellowship.

Diligence Brings Rewards

I want to look at Isaac's life to see if his future was secured by his father's blessings:

> *And Isaac was forty years old when he took Rebekah to wife, ... And Isaac intreated the LORD for his wife, because she was barren: and the LORD was intreated of him, and Rebekah his wife conceived.*

> Genesis 25:20,21

Doesn't this sound familiar? Isaac's mother had been barren, and now his wife, Rebekah, was barren. What did Isaac do? He interceded to God on Rebekah's behalf. No doubt Abraham and Sarah had shared their testimony again and again of how God had blessed them with their miracle baby, Isaac. They had secured Isaac's future by sharing their faith with him. When Isaac was confronted with a similar problem, he knew enough about spiritual things to pray and believe God for a child.

Allowing our children to see us walking diligently in faith and conducting our lives according to godly wisdom is the best example we can set because it sets the tone for their spiritual growth. You can see the principle of sowing and reaping in action here. If you sow spiritual things like faith and godly wisdom into your children's future, then they will reap a future rooted in faith and godly wisdom. However, when you sow worldly things like chance and luck, your children's future will be rooted in that same kind of instability.

We simply cannot pass along to our children what we do not have ourselves. So if you need wisdom (and, quite frankly, we all do), ask God. Then begin to seek

Him more through prayer and reading His Word. You will be pleasantly surprised at the difference godly wisdom makes in your life today—and in your future.

One of my favorite Scriptures is, "But without faith it is impossible to please him: for he that cometh to God must believe that he is, and that he is a rewarder of them that diligently seek him" (Hebrews 11:6).

I pray this Scripture regularly during my prayer times. I have certain things that I am believing God for, but sometimes the answer (reward) seems to take forever. So I continue to remind myself that God is a rewarder of them who diligently seek Him. When I set aside a daily time to spend with God, I know He is going to reward me for the time I spend with Him.

Let me encourage you to be diligent in seeking God— that's wisdom!

Maybe you need victory in your life, or perhaps your spouse or your children or someone else close to you have some problem areas they need to overcome. Let me encourage you to be diligent in seeking God—that's wisdom! And when you continue to pray and trust God, He will reward you and your loved ones will be blessed to live victorious lives. Remember, diligence brings reward; and lack of diligence brings nothing.

If you want to Satan-proof your loved ones, then you will need to set aside a special time each day for prayer—genuine prayer that seeks God. Then not only will He reward you with His presence, but God also will bless you because you spent time seeking Him. Wow! That's a double-portion blessing! In addition, when you allow your children to see that spending time in God's presence is a primary part of your life, they too will begin to understand the importance of living in faith and walking in godly wisdom.

There is a woman I know who is such an inspiration because she has tremendous faith for the salvation of her loved ones. This woman is absolutely determined that all of them are coming into the kingdom of God. She spends much time seeking God's wisdom, which she really needs because it takes godly wisdom to live with an unsaved mate.

This woman's bulldog faith secured her son's future when he was a senior in high school. All through his high school years, the young man had pretty much fooled around. Although he was very bright and was capable of getting good grades, he never quite hit the mark. Then in his last semester of school, the boy told his parents that he didn't really feel like going to school—he had given up hope of succeeding.

Despite his academic performance, my friend encouraged her son to stay in school—she was absolutely convinced of his ability to graduate with his class. She told him, "In Genesis it says that all men are made in the image and likeness of God. Son, I don't care what anybody says about you; I choose right now to see the image of God in you. That's all I am going to look at."

This mother had faith in God for her son, and she walked in godly wisdom and applied the Word to the situation. The young man decided to return to school, and God sent a Christian teacher to encourage him.

I believe this mother's supernatural faith secured her son's academic future because soon he began to have confidence in himself. He began to work diligently, carrying a full load plus one extra class; and he graduated from high school with his head held high.

The woman Satan-proofed her son by securing his future, and the results were victorious. In the future, if the boy should ever happen to become discouraged, I believe he will remember his mother's example; and God will bring him through difficult times again and again.

Let's look back at how Abraham's example of godly wisdom and faith took root in Isaac's life. When Isaac became old and was nearing death, he followed his father's example and blessed his children. I believe there is wisdom in blessing our children with our substance as well as with our mouths. So many parents have the attitude, "I never had it easy. I've always worked and earned my way; let my children do the same."

I agree wholeheartedly that our children should be responsible for themselves, but I also know that we need to prepare our children to live independently. I believe it is very wise for parents to have insurance so their children will have the resources to pay for college educations in case the parents die. Educational security is an important part of securing the future for your children and your grandchildren.

Isaac saw the wisdom in his father's actions, and he wanted to do the same for his two sons Jacob and Esau. Isaac called Esau in and said, "Esau, go cook me some savory meat, because I want to bless you before I die" (see Genesis 27:4). Esau probably was very excited. Remember, he had already lost his birthright blessing through his own foolishness; and he had no intention of losing the firstborn blessing as well. So he ran out to kill the meat he needed to make a stew for his aging father.

All this seems to be very much in order except for one thing. Isaac was not walking in godly wisdom. You only can operate in godly wisdom when you are living according to God's Word:

> *And the Lord said unto her, Two nations are in thy womb, and two man-ner of people shall be separated from thy bowels; and the one people shall be stronger than the other people; and the elder shall serve the younger.*

> Genesis 25:23

Blessing Esau was not what God had said to Rebekah. Rather, when these twin boys were still in her womb, God had said that the younger son would be blessed. The younger son was Jacob, not Esau; so despite Isaac's seemingly good intentions, he simply was out of God's will. The firstborn blessing had to do with rulership, prosperity, and priestly authority. Isaac was very unwise to try to secure the future of his household by choosing to give that blessing to Esau when God's choice was Jacob. Isaac's ungodly actions nearly resulted in his younger son's death, because Esau certainly wanted to kill Jacob.

As I said earlier, Jacob had to flee for his life, and he went to live with his Uncle Laban. Poor Jacob had such a hard time. Laban changed Jacob's wages ten times and tricked him into marrying Leah when Jacob really loved Rachel. But one thing I noticed, Jacob always came out smelling like a rose! Why? Because his father had secured his future by prophesying the blessings of God on Jacob's life.

Friend, we can have faith for our children's future. When we parents begin to walk in faith and to govern our actions by godly wisdom, then God's bless-ings will come upon our lives and our children's lives as well.

There is absolutely no question that you will reap what you sow. Maybe it will be a fast crop, and you'll reap it tomorrow or a month from now; or maybe your children will reap what you have sown long after your death. But you will always secure your future when you sow seeds of faith in God's Word. God's Word contains over 7,000 promises; and when God brings His Word to pass, there is always a harvest or manifestation of a promise.

Blessed by Faith

Jacob knew that his future was secure. Why? Because Isaac had blessed him. Despite the trickery involved, Jacob's future was secured when Isaac blessed him by faith. (Certainly it was not by sight, because Isaac thought he was blessing Esau instead of Jacob.) This should give us all confidence to know that God will do all He possibly can to manifest His plans for our lives. Even if we don't have the perfect family or background, we can secure our future in God's will.

When we look at how Isaac's behavior affected Jacob's life, I want you to notice how the principle of sowing and reaping worked in their lives. Remember how Isaac's favorite son was Esau and Rebekah's favorite son was Jacob? Well, Jacob carried on that same behavior; his favorite son was Joseph: "Now Israel [Jacob] loved Joseph more than all his children..." (Genesis 37:3).

Favoritism certainly brought heartaches for Jacob's entire family. Joseph's brothers were jealous of him because of their father's preferential treatment, and they actually hated Joseph because he had a dream in which he was in authority over them:

> *And his brethren said to him, Shalt thou indeed reign over us? or shalt thou indeed have dominion over us? And they hated him yet the more for his dreams, and for his words.*

> Genesis 37:8

Finally, the brothers took Joseph and threw him into a pit. They killed a goat, put its blood on Joseph's special multi-colored coat, took the coat to their father, and told him Joseph had been killed by a wild animal. In reality, they had sold their own brother into slavery (see Genesis 37:28).

Did you notice that Jacob's sons were using a method similar to that which Jacob had used to deceive Isaac—an animal skin? You can sow wrong things in your future too. Jacob sowed some wrong things, and his whole family suffered because he did not walk in godly wisdom.

But Joseph is another success story—he stayed true to God throughout his whole life and became the key to rescuing them during the great famine (see Genesis 45:7). Joseph finally revealed his identity to his family and treated them like kings. Joseph had lived his whole life in faith; he walked in much godly wisdom; and he certainly secured the future for his family.

Joseph's life is a wonderful testimony of how we believers can maintain our faith in God's Word. We can walk in godly wisdom even when our circumstances fail us. We can Satan-proof our lives by walking in righteousness and holiness. We can pray that our children will never be conformed to the world but that they will transform the world. That's God's wisdom to us. Joseph was a very wise man, and he definitely made a difference in the lives of an entire nation.

I believe seeing Joseph walk in godly wisdom really blessed Jacob, whose name by now had been changed to *Israel*, which means "one who prevails with God and man." And when Israel neared the end of his life, he secured his loved ones' future:

> *And it came to pass after these things, that one told Joseph, Behold, thy father is sick: and he took with him his two sons, Manasseh and Ephraim.... And he said, Bring them, I pray thee, unto me, and I will bless them.*

> Genesis 48:1,9

But when Israel began to pray for his grandsons, he did something very strange:

"And Israel stretched out his right hand, and laid it upon Ephraim's head, who was the younger, and his left hand upon Manasseh's head..." (Genesis 48:14). Israel began to bless Joseph and said, "...God, before whom my fathers Abraham and Isaac did walk, the God which fed me all my life long unto this day" (Genesis 48:15). Israel went on to tell Joseph how his seed would be blessed.

But Joseph became a little disturbed when he noticed that his father was giving the firstborn blessing to Ephraim instead of Manasseh, who was the oldest (see Genesis 48:17,18). Joseph tried to correct his father, but Israel stood firm in his blessing. And in studying the history of Ephraim, I found that when he got into the Promised Land, his tribe grew so much that the Ephraimites covered the land more than any one other tribe. Manasseh wasn't too far behind him, but Ephraim prospered the most. Why? Because Ephraim's future had been secured by Israel, who in his latter years began to walk in faith and in godly wisdom.

Now when Joseph neared his death, I was puzzled by what he said:

And Joseph took an oath of the children of Israel, saying, God will surely visit you, and ye shall carry up my bones from hence .

Genesis 50:25

At one time I was troubled by this strange request, but God showed me that Joseph knew the Israelites were going to be in Egypt for over four hundred years. How? Genesis 15 tells us that Abraham entered into covenant with God, and God said He would deliver Abraham's seed out of Egypt. Abraham shared God's Word with Isaac, Isaac shared God's Word with Jacob, and Jacob shared God's Word with his children. Based on his faith in God and the testimony of God's Word about the Israelites, Joseph had faith for the future of an entire nation. And I want you to know that when the Israelites were delivered from bondage in Egypt, they carried Joseph's bones with them. They carried those bones around in the wilderness for forty years. They didn't have the written Word—but they certainly had the assurance that their future had been secured.

Now let's review the three blessings for your future: material, inheritance, and victory. Just as Abraham blessed Isaac with all his substance, God also wants to bless His people with material blessings. He wants you to be blessed and to prosper. Why? So you can be a blessing to the kingdom of God. When you sow financial seeds into God's kingdom, you can expect to reap financial blessings in return.

The same thing holds true for prayer. If you will sacrifice time each day for prayer not only for yourself, but also for your loved ones, someone will inherit the deposit you are making in your prayer account. And if you sow prayers, you will reap answers in your own life.

Lastly, God wants His people to have faith for future victories. When you begin to Satan-proof your life and the lives of others by walking in faith and in godly wisdom, you will get a clearer understanding of the hope we have in Jesus Christ: "Who shall change our vile body, that it may be fashioned like unto his glorious body, according to the working whereby he is able even to subdue all things unto himself" (Philippians 3:21).

If the only hope we had was in this life, then we'd all be miserable people. But if you have been born again, then your hope is not in this life or in this body. The Bible says that Jesus is going to raise our bodies and make them like His! (1 Corinthians 6:14; 1 John 3:2.) So, despite the circumstances around you, get excited because through Jesus Christ, God has secured the future for all of His children throughout eternity.

—⊰•⊱—

CHAPTER 9

Be a Light Reflector

Now I want to look at how Satan-proofers can turn on the light wherever there is darkness. You know, at one time every one of us was in darkness: "For ye were sometimes darkness, but now are ye light in the Lord: walk as children of the light" (Ephesians 5:8).

In this verse, the apostle Paul was exhorting the Christians not to be partakers of the sinful lifestyle from which they had been delivered. The same holds true for us today. Sometimes we try to "measure" the depth of the darkness in which we may have been involved. On our "rating scale," we consider some types of darkness to be "greater" than others. Nevertheless, the Word of God warns all of us not to return to the lifestyles we were involved in before we accepted Jesus Christ as our Lord and Savior.

When you were born again, God destined you to be conformed into the image of Jesus Christ (see Romans 8:29). An image is a reflection—you are being made to be a reflection of Jesus, the Light of the world (see John 3:19; 9:5). You're not the actual Light itself, but you are a Light reflector. Look at the sun and the stars: although they may seem to be the source of light for the planet earth, actually the sun and stars are merely reflectors. The source of light is the same as the source of everything—the Word of God (see Genesis 1:3).

The same is true for us; we are people who have been destined to be Satan-proofers by reflecting God's Word and His will on the earth.

I want you to see how you can walk in God's light and change the circumstances around you. You can Satan-proof your circumstances when you allow God's light to shine forth in your relationships with other people.

When Jesus comes into our hearts and we begin to allow ourselves to be conformed into His image, we become instruments God can use to reflect His light—His Word and His will. As we continue to grow in our relationship with the Lord, He will give us more opportunities to reflect His light (Word and will) in the lives of other people. Also, there will be many times when you'll meet people who will turn on the light for you. There may come a time when you will be surrounded by the darkness of uncertainty, or lack of faith. You won't know what to do next about your circumstances, and that's when God will send another believer who will turn on the light for you.

I remember some years ago, we were trying to get a loan for a new church building. It was very difficult because, at that time, Denver banks were not loaning money to churches. The building we had moved from hadn't sold right away; and even if it had, the money would not have been nearly enough to meet this new challenge. We had sort of a "rent to own" agreement on the new building; and if we couldn't meet our first month's obligation, the cost of the building would go up by $120,000!

This was a very dark time for our ministry. Wally and I were certain that the Lord had led us to acquire a new building; but the finances just didn't seem to be available. Then, one of our church members came up and said, "I believe we can get a loan."

For eight months this man went from bank to bank trying to get financing. When we would ask him about his progress, he would respond, "No, not yet; but we are going to get a loan!" He kept the light turned on for us. And two weeks before the closing, two banks said yes! We got the loan the day before we would have had to pay the $120,000 increase!

What helped us to get through this stressful period? One of God's Light reflectors! Our friend was moving in supernatural faith—the faith of Christ—for this situation, and God certainly performed a miracle on our behalf.

How about you? Can you remember a time when you turned on the Light through standing in faith and in prayer with someone during a time when their situation looked hopeless? Or perhaps you may have been the one who faced a difficult situation that seemed to be beyond your level of faith. Does our loving heavenly Father leave us alone during those stressful periods? *No!* God will send someone to turn on the Light—someone to stand on God's Word with you and to pray so His will can be done in your life.

The Bible tells how Seth turned on the Light after Abel was killed by their brother Cain. Abel was supposed to be the one who carried the line from Adam and Eve. You could say that, in a sense, Abel was the seed of promise—the light. Can you imagine what would have happened if we all would have been descendants of an ungodly man such as Cain? Thank God that Adam and Eve had another son Seth:

And Adam knew his wife again; and she bare a son, and called his name Seth: For God, said she, hath appointed me another seed instead of Abel, whom Cain slew.

Genesis 4:25

During the time of Seth's son Enos, men began to call upon the name of the Lord. Why? Because Seth became a Light reflector—he was a godly man who had taught his family how to pray, and they turned on the Light for that next generation.

Let me tell you, God will never let His Light go out! He will always have men and women whom He can use to manifest His Word and will on the earth. Satan-proofers are just believers who turn on God's Light in every situation in which they become involved.

Turn on God's Light

When I think about a light, I can't help thinking about Noah. He lived during a time when it seemed as though God absolutely had become fed up with everybody! People were involved in all types of sin—the women had even become sexually involved with fallen angels, and the children of these ungodly unions were giants (see Genesis 6:2,4). God was so disgusted by all the terrible things they were doing that He was sorry He had ever created man:

...I will destroy man whom I have created from the face of the earth...for it repenteth me that I have made them.

Genesis 6:7

Sometimes, I think we get so upset when we think about the terrible conditions in which we live. But let me ask you, when is the last time you saw a giant walking around? You might be experiencing some problems with your unsaved husband or wife, but at least you aren't married to one of the wicked angels who had been kicked out of heaven along with Satan! Yet, in Noah's day, these things were common.

It's no wonder that God became fed up! And just when it looked as though it could have been "curtains" for the inhabitants of the earth, Noah found favor with God; and he and his family were spared from destruction: "But Noah found grace in the eyes of the Lord" (Genesis 6:8).

Out of the entire human race, only Noah and his family allowed themselves to reflect God's Word and His will. Noah loved God, he led his family in the ways of God, and they certainly turned on God's light during that dark period in history.

When you think about becoming a Satan-proofer—someone who turns on God's Light in the world—you might think, "Well, I'm not important; I'm just one person." However, just as one candle can light up a dark room, so can one believer light up a dark situation.

You may be the only one in your family who is a reflector of God's wonderful Word and His will. Just hang in there; because if you don't turn on the Light for your own loved ones, who will? Even if you become discouraged with them or with yourself, remember that God has placed you there to keep His Light turned on in their lives.

One of our care group leaders shared that, at one time, he had lived with a woman to whom he was not married. These two had been brought up in the church, but they had turned their backs on the Lord and had begun to live a worldly lifestyle. One day, God sent a believer who really turned on God's

Light in that dark situation. The woman was invited to attend one of our services at Orchard Road Christian Center; and while she attended church, he stayed home to watch football.

She was born again and Spirit-filled, then she turned on the light in her home. Her boyfriend became born again and Spirit-filled; they were married and now have three beautiful children. They have a wonderful ministry in our care groups, and he recently has entered into full-time ministry!

How did this happen? Because one person obeyed God, and God used this believer to turn on His Light in this couple's life. I love the way God gets so much mileage out of just one believer who is willing to reflect the light of Jesus in the world.

Someone else who reflected God's Light was Joseph. He certainly kept God's Light turned on for Israel, as well as for Egypt. The nation of Israel was still a small family at this time—just Israel's (Jacob's) household, which was composed of about 70 people. As we saw earlier, Joseph had been separated from his family because his brothers had become so jealous and evil that they sold him into slavery. Joseph endured terrible hardships and temptations; but Joseph didn't give in to Potiphar's wife, he didn't give in to the pressures of prison, and he didn't give in to bitterness toward his brothers.

No, Joseph stayed true to God; and God gave him a plan to save Egypt and that whole Middle East area during a tremendous famine. Joseph's family survived because he kept God's Light burning. If there ever comes a time when you begin to feel unimportant, just remember Joseph and keep turning on God's Light wherever you go. There have been so many men like Joseph who allowed themselves to be used by God to turn a particular situation around.

Moses was another one. When God spoke to Moses and told him to get the Israelites delivered out of Egypt, first, Moses completely blew it. He did everything all wrong and had to go out in the desert to get some more training. For 40 years Moses cared for his father-in-law Jethro's sheep; that certainly was an effective training ground for one who would pastor the entire nation of Israel (which had grown to about two million by now).

Finally, God commissioned Moses to go down to Egypt and deal with Pharaoh about releasing the Israelites from slavery. Moses and Aaron obeyed

God, and they definitely turned on God's Light. Through a series of miracles, God began to deal with Pharaoh. Eventually the people were set free.

Stand in Prayer

Moses led the Israelites on what turned out to be a 40-year journey through the wilderness. Moses really had plenty of opportunities to turn on God's Light for these people. Those people just murmured and complained the whole time they were in the wilderness. So much so, that the entire generation, except for Joshua and Caleb, died in the wilderness without ever getting to cross over into the Promised Land.

I think Moses' life gives us insight as to how God wants believers to respond when our loved ones seem to want to stay in the darkness of sin. One time, when Moses had gone up on Mount Sinai to talk with God, the people became very impatient because Moses had been gone so long. They told Aaron to make them a golden calf. God said to Moses, "I am so disgusted with them I want to wipe the whole crowd out and start over with you" (see Exodus 32:10).

How did Moses respond? He could have said, "Well, God, that's a good idea, because all they do is murmur and whine around." But he didn't; instead, Moses said, "God, if you blot them out, then blot me out too." One man saved the whole nation of Israel. How? By standing in prayer, he turned on God's Light for the people.

Just as Moses turned on God's Light for the children of Israel through prayer, so can we pray God's Light into each other's circumstances. A while back, we were going through a very difficult time with our son. Michael had gotten involved with drugs, and he had begun trying to involve some of the young people of the church in drugs. This was a very dark time for Wally and me. The devil would taunt us, saying things like, "Why are you in the ministry? Even your own child isn't serving God. Who are you to get up and preach to the people? What is the church going to say about you? What are people going to say about you?"

Well, Wally and I just told our members the truth. We said, "We're having a hard time. Our son is in trouble, and we're in trouble. Will you please pray for us?" I never heard any criticism. They were absolutely fantastic and said, "We're going to pray for you, we're going to fast for you, and we're going to hold on to God's Word for you." Our congregation kept the Light turned on for us. It's no wonder that we think Orchard Road Christian Center members are so wonderful!

Another one of my favorite light reflectors is Gideon. I know that sometimes we tend to look down on Gideon because when the angel first came to him, Gideon was so pitiful. But the angel saw Gideon in God's image—as a Light reflector:

> *... The LORD is with thee, thou mighty man of valour.*

> Judges 6:12

Gideon's response was something like, "Who me? Do you know about me? I have a low I.Q., my family is poor, and we live on the wrong side of the tracks." Gideon's self-esteem was literally in the pits. But the angel didn't pay any heed to Gideon's low opinion of himself. He said, "Gideon, you and God can rid the land of the Midianites" (see Judges 6:16).

Now during this time, it looked like all of Israel was going to be wiped out by the Midianites; and it certainly didn't look like Gideon was capable of doing anything to stop them. Yet Gideon continued to listen to God, and God continued to deal with Gideon. Finally, God sent Gideon out to fight the Midianites with only 300 men. You say, "Three-hundred men against a whole army? They must have had some very powerful weapons!"

You'll be surprised to know that they only had four types of weapons: trumpets, pitchers, lamps, and swords (see Judges 7:16). They blew the trumpets, took the sword, hit the pitcher, and the light sprang forth as they shouted, "The sword of the Lord and of Gideon!" This little band of soldiers absolutely defeated the fierce Midianite army. How? By carrying God's Light.

How often do we allow opportunities to *turn on God's light* to slip away because we are afraid? You may look at yourself and say, "Well, I've never attended Bible school, I didn't graduate from high school, I don't have any experience, I'm not good looking, I've got a big nose, I say the wrong things, or I just can't do it!" But that is a lie from the devil because you can do all things through Christ, who strengthens you (see Philippians 4:13).

Despite your shortcomings and faults, God can use you to turn on His Light in the circumstances around you. Look at all the men I have mentioned. They all had faults, but they were willing to listen to God; and as they began to respond to God, He used them to turn their situations around.

It's a tremendous blessing when God allows you to turn on the Light in a dark situation. It's also a blessing when God sends someone to turn on the Light for you. One time about seven or eight years ago, I felt like some of my staff were just going to quit the ministry because they may have thought I had made some wrong decisions. One young woman came to me crying; I thought she had come to quit. So I asked, "Are you going to quit?" She said, "Quit? No! God called me here; and although I may not understand everything you do, I have confidence in you." Let me tell you, her encouragement meant so much to me; it was as if she had turned the light back on for me.

I want you to know that you won't always be aware when you have turned on the Light for someone. That's why we must be so cautious to be led by the Holy Spirit in our dealings with people. Sometimes God's loving Light may shine through someone's darkness because of your smile, your prayers, or your kind words. Turning on God's Light doesn't always have to be through some big thing. For the most part, God's Light will shine in the little things that we do.

I read an interesting description about a glowworm. The steps it takes are so small, they can hardly be measured. And as the glowworm moves across a field at midnight, it produces just enough light in its glow to illuminate one single step forward. So as the glowworm moves ahead, it always moves into light.

Sometimes God will allow you to bless others in a way that will produce very obvious results in their lives. But, usually God will allow you to be like the glowworm. You'll turn God's Light on during someone's dark moments or moods, and little by little they will begin to move into God's direction for their lives.

Keep the Light Burning

You know, sometimes God's Light may be turned on by the most unexpected people, such as the child Samuel. He came on the scene during a very pitiful situation. Samuel probably expected Eli to be the one who would turn on the Light. After all, Eli was the high priest, who was supposed to instruct Samuel in the priesthood. But, sadly, Eli was not obedient to God's instructions concerning childrearing. Eli had two sons, Hophni and Phinehas, whom he had so indulged that he hadn't disciplined or trained them. They were involved in adultery, and they were stealing from the sacrifices (see 1 Samuel 2:12-16,22).

It certainly looked like God's Light for Israel's spiritual atmosphere was about to go out. However, instead of Eli turning on the Light for Israel, Samuel was God's man for the occasion.

Even as a young boy, God had begun to talk to Samuel and Samuel had begun to listen to God's voice (see 1 Samuel 3:4-14). Samuel didn't become rebellious toward Eli and say, "You're a poor example to me; how can I be a believer? And look at your kids; they're the pits." No, Samuel kept holding on to God's Word.

Later when Israel was attacked by the Philistines (see 1 Samuel 4:1), the Ark of God was taken and both Eli's sons were killed in battle. When Eli heard the news, "...he fell from off the seat backward by the side of the gate, and his neck brake, and he died: for he was an old man, and heavy. And he had judged Israel forty years" (1 Samuel 4:18).

And there is something else that happened to Eli's son. Phinehas' wife was pregnant and went into labor when the news came. Evidently, she was not in good health because when her son was born, she was near death (see 1 Samuel 4:20). She completely ignored her son:

And she named the child Ichabod, saying, The glory is departed from Israel....

1 Samuel 4:21

She thought God's Light had been turned off, but she was wrong. The glory of God hadn't departed from Israel. Do you know why? Because Samuel had God's Light on the inside of him.

It doesn't matter who blows it or backslides; that is not our problem. A Satan-proofer will keep God's Light on. Jesus is the Light, and He is inside every believer. If we will stand in His Light, who knows what we can do for those who backslide or blow it!

A woman called in one day with a praise report. Previously she had requested prayer because her son's girlfriend was pregnant and was scheduled to have an abortion. However, a Christian friend began to pray with the girl and helped her to understand that abortion was wrong. Praise God, the girl-friend changed her mind and decided to keep her baby.

Friend, when we pray for each other, we are turning on God's Light.

❧

I don't know whether this girl has received Christ or not; but I do know that her Christian friend has turned on God's Light in this dark situation. And I believe the son, the girlfriend, and the baby are all going to become born again and Spirit-filled.

Friend, when we pray for each other, we are turning on God's Light. I love to turn on God's Light for other people. Don't you? Wouldn't you rather pray and bring forth God's Word and His will in people's lives than to turn God's Light off by participating in gossip and strife? Well, evidently Samuel chose to keep the Light on for Israel; and the nation didn't go under because God's Light shined through Samuel.

When I travel, sometimes people come to me with all kinds of stories about troublesome leadership in their churches. I always challenge them to be Satan-proofers. I ask, "Well, are you standing in faith? Are you praying? Or are you criticizing and being negative?" Sometimes I think that God allows us to see problems so we can pray and keep the Light turned on until He turns the situation around.

Another place I have seen people turn on God's Light is for marriages that look like they are falling apart. One mate will keep God's Light burning, and many of those marriages are standing strong today. Why? Because one believing mate refuses to let God's Light go out for his or her marriage.

There was another time in Israel's history when it looked like the Light of God's spiritual atmosphere was about to go out. A king named Jehoram had married a wicked woman named Athaliah—she is absolutely the worst woman in the Bible. You may be thinking, "No, Jezebel is the worst." Well, Athaliah was Jezebel's daughter; and I think Athaliah was much better at being evil than Jezebel.

After Athaliah's husband died, their son Ahaziah took the throne of Judah and was killed while visiting the king of Israel. Athaliah wanted the throne so much that she ordered the murder of her own grandchildren (see 2 Kings 11:1). This woman certainly was the pits! Her actions could have eliminated all hope for the Messiah to come forth from the house of David. This would have been absolutely devastating for Israel and for you and me (the Body of Christ) as well!

But God had a provision for this critical situation. God's provision came in the form of a priest named Jehoiada, who had married Athaliah's daughter Jehosheba. When his mother-in-law began to murder all the children, Jehosheba slipped in, took the only remaining grandchild, Joash, and hid him from his wicked grandmother (see 2 Kings 11:2). I really admire Jehosheba's courage and her desire to do God's will, even though it meant going against her mother, who was quite capable of killing Jehosheba in the process.

But Jehosheba probably said something like, "God will take care of me. If I perish, I perish; but the light cannot go out for the house of David." So, she stole that little tiny baby and hid him in her home for six years. She and Jehoiada raised Joash; and when he was seven years old, they secretly took him into the Temple to be crowned the rightful king of Israel:

And when Athaliah heard the noise of the guard and of the people, she came to the people into the temple of the LORD.

2 Kings 11:13

In the midst of the celebration, Athaliah came running down the aisle crying, "Treason, treason":

And they laid hands on her; and she went by the way by the which the horses came into the king's house: and there was she slain.

2 Kings 11:16

127

The good news is, despite all the devil's attempts, God's Light will never go out! He will always have men and women—Satan-proofers—who will say, "God, I am going to stay true to You and turn Your Light on in this situation."

I'll give you another example of someone who reflected God's will— Daniel. While Daniel was enslaved in Babylon, he turned on God's Light for three kings: Nebuchadnezzar, Belshazzar, and Darius. Daniel had favor with God in the area of interpreting dreams and visions. Now Daniel could have sold out and turned away from God's people; after all, they had been taken into captivity because of their own sin. But Daniel stayed true to God and to God's people, and he prayed for the Jews. Then one night something very strange happened while King Belshazzar was having a big drunken brawl:

> *In the same hour came forth fingers of a man's hand, and wrote ...upon the plaister of the wall of the king's palace....*

Daniel 5:5

Can you imagine how unusual that must have been? Suddenly a hand appeared out of nowhere and began to write on the wall. Well, Belshazzar was simply terrified:

> *Then the king's countenance was changed, and his thoughts troubled him, so that the joints of his loins were loosed, and his knees smote one against another.*

Daniel 5:6

I think it's almost funny! Here Belshazzar was making a mockery out of God by allowing the golden vessels that were taken out of the Temple to be used as drinking containers at this party. But what happened when the hand of God appeared? Belshazzar's face became pale, his whole body began to tremble, and his knees started knocking!

None of the king's astrologers or soothsayers knew what had been written. In fact, there was only one person in the entire kingdom who could interpret the handwriting on the wall. That's right—Daniel was the only man who could turn on God's light for that situation. Friend, when you look around you and see all the trouble in the world, don't get nervous because it can't be that dark if you're around. You are a Satan-proofer—God's provision for the situation. All you have to do is to turn on God's light wherever you go.

The last person I want to tell you about is Saul (Paul): "And as he journeyed, he came near Damascus: and suddenly there shined round about him a light from heaven" (Acts 9:3).

Before Saul met Jesus, he was in darkness. Even though he may have loved God, he was trying to serve God with his mind and his legalistic teaching. However, God wanted Paul to turn on His Light and so God sent the Light—Jesus—to Paul. After Paul had received the Light of Christ, God made him a light to the Gentiles (Acts 13:47). God sent Paul to preach to the Gentiles, and that was the beginning of a tremendous revival that would extend all the way down to you and me.

I want to tell you that just as Paul was a Light reflector, you and I are Light reflectors too. Jesus is the Light of the world; and although we believers are not the actual Light itself, we reflect the Word and the will of the marvelous Light who dwells inside us. Through the power of God, we can be Satan-proofers as we reflect God's Word and His will throughout the earth.

CHAPTER 10

The Power to Transform

I am sure that you all want to see your loved ones go forward; you want to see your spouse, your children, and the rest of those you care for really begin to walk victoriously in the Lord. So when they are suffering, wounded, or defeated, it hurts you too, doesn't it? It hurts when you know your loved ones are not walking in the victory available for them in Jesus Christ.

However, as Satan-proofers we are not going to focus upon the hurts; we are going to focus on Jesus Christ! By faith, we are going to take authority over their situations and begin to operate in God's transforming power for our loved ones. That is the purpose of a Satan-proofer—to transform the circumstances around you (subdue the earth).

God never intended for us to sit passively by and watch the devil cover the earth with destruction. That's why God gave believers authority over the devil:

Behold, I give unto you power to tread on serpents and scorpions and over all the power of the enemy: and nothing shall by any means hurt you.

Luke 10:19

In a previous chapter, we saw that the first time the word *power* appears in this verse refers to "authority," and the second time *power* appears here refers

131

to "miracle-working power." You received God's authority the moment you were born again; and if you have been baptized in the Holy Spirit, you have been given God's miracle-working power. What are you supposed to do with God's authority and power? Stop Satan from wreaking havoc in the area where you have influence.

There was a woman from Chicago, who had been participating in our Bible-reading plan. She wrote that her son had been classified by the police as a habitual criminal—he was hopelessly locked into a criminal mindset. But praise God, as she began to feed herself with God's Word, it began to change her from being hopeless to hopeful about her son:

> *Though hand join in hand, the wicked shall not be unpunished: but the seed of the righteous shall be delivered.*
>
> Proverbs 11:21

This woman had gotten ahold of God's Word concerning a promise for her son. She began to Satan-proof her child and reminded God of His Word, "Father, You promised me that my seed will be delivered." Let me tell you, God's Word is transforming power and it absolutely reversed the course of her son's life.

This diligent mother stood on Proverbs 11:21. She began to meditate on it, she spoke it out loud, and she prayed it. During the testimony service at her church, she boldly proclaimed, "I know God is going to save my son, and he will preach the gospel in this church."

Of course, the other members thought, "You poor, deluded woman. Your son is always going to be the pits." Yet, she said, "Marilyn, I didn't let the dirty looks affect me, I just held onto God's Word." She had focused all her attention on God's Word—His transforming power.

One night at ten o'clock, she felt an unusual burden to pray in tongues for her son. He called her (long distance) an hour later, asking what she had been doing between 10:00 and 10:30 that night. He had sold some bad drugs to a man who had come to his apartment during that time, and the man had beat him to a pulp. The man pulled out a gun intending to shoot my friend's son; but whenever he tried to pull the trigger, his finger would not bend! He tried several times, but he just couldn't do it. Finally he threw the gun down and ran out saying, "Your mother is doing something to stop me from pulling this trigger!" Imagine, this gunman knew that his intended victim's mother was somehow stopping him from killing her son!

She had been praying God's Word for her son—God's transforming power. When the son came home, he was born again, Spirit-filled, attended Bible school, and was invited to be the guest speaker at their church.

You see, your loved ones can be transformed! If they are living a life that is filled with hopelessness and despair, then it's because they are living outside of God's will. God's will is His Word. It is His transforming power, and it can have tremendous consequences in your life as well as in the lives of those you care for.

I am going to give you some things to consider as you begin to Satan-proof your life and those you love through God's transforming power: the father's faith, it's time for our loved ones to arise, the mother's faith, power to transform the past, and catching the faith vision for your loved ones. While the focus of these will be on children, the godly principles I'm going to share can be applied to others in your life as well.

Consider: The Father's Faith

We're going to look first at the faith of fathers: "So Jesus came again into Cana of Galilee, where he made the water wine. And there was a certain nobleman, whose son was sick at Capernaum" (John 4:46).

This man was a Gentile and was very prosperous. This man's son was very, very ill; and no one expected the child to live. Although the nobleman was not a believer, he was so moved by compassion for his son that he found Jesus and asked Him to heal the boy. Jesus didn't respond favorably to his first plea and called the man a sign-seeker. But when the nobleman asked Him again, Jesus responded: "Go thy way; thy son liveth..." (John 4:50).

This child had a problem; he was almost dying—and this father took his son to Jesus—not physically, but by faith. What are fathers supposed to do when their children have problems? Do they become nervous, start biting their nails, and pulling out their hair? No! Do they say, "Oh, I'm letting my wife handle our children"? *No!*

What happened when that nobleman took his son, by faith, to Jesus? Jesus spoke the Word, which is God's transforming power, and the boy was miraculously healed. And not only was the child healed, the whole family was born again! The transforming power of Jesus Christ always does more than we can ask or think. All we need do is to get ahold of God's Word and begin to apply it to our circumstances.

Just hearing Jesus speak the Word increased the nobleman's faith so much that instead of running home to see if his son had been healed, the man went about his business and didn't go home until the next day. He had gotten ahold of God's Word—His transforming power—and the man's faith skyrocketed right into the supernatural.

So then faith cometh by hearing, and hearing by the word of God.

Romans 10:17

When the nobleman finally did go home, his servants rushed out to meet him. They said, "Guess what happened? Your son is healed!" The man asked the servants to pinpoint the exact hour that his son began to recover. They told him, and it was the same hour Jesus had spoken the words of healing. And, you know, just as God's transforming power worked in this family, it will work for your family and other loved ones today!

You may think, "Well, my children aren't sick." But perhaps you suspect your son or daughter (or someone else you care about) of being involved in drugs, alcohol, or illicit sex. Or, maybe you have evidence that your children have become involved in the occult. You say, "I've talked to them and done everything I can think of; but my children won't listen to me." Hang on, and listen to how one man dealt with a similar problem:

There came to him [Jesus] a certain man, kneeling down to him [Jesus], and saying, Lord, have mercy on my son: for he is lunatick, and sore vexed: for oftentimes he falleth into the fire, and oft into the water.

Matthew 17:14,15

Now this boy had a spiritual need—deliverance. What did Jesus do when He was confronted with this tormented child, who was under such a tense level of demonic oppression that he literally was falling into fire and water? Did Jesus back off from this boy's problems? No way: "And Jesus rebuked the devil; and he [the devil] departed out of him: and the child was cured from that very hour" (v. 18).

Jesus spoke the Word and completely turned the boy's circumstances around, and He'll do the same thing for your loved ones too. You can make the difference in your loved ones' lives if you will take them, by faith, to Jesus and receive His transforming power for their situations.

Consider: It's Time for Our Loved Ones to Arise

Sometimes when we read about healings or deliverances, the devil may begin to play tricks in our minds. We find ourselves thinking, *Yeah, Jesus may have been able to handle that situation; but it's not nearly as bad as mine.* Well, let me show you something that will wipe out all your excuses:

And behold, there cometh one of the rulers of the synagogue Jairus by name; and when he saw him [Jesus], he fell at his feet, And besought him greatly saying, My little daughter lieth at the point of death: I pray thee, come and lay thy hands on her, that she may be healed; and she shall live.

Mark 5:22,23

Here we see a father named Jairus coming to Jesus on behalf of his deathly sick child. I looked up *Jairus* and found the name means "He shall enlighten." After his encounter with Jesus, Jairus certainly became enlightened to the transforming power of God's Word. He found out that it is never too late for Jesus to turn negative circumstances around.

On His way to heal Jairus' daughter, Jesus stopped to heal a woman who had been hemorrhaging for 12 years. While Jesus was talking to this woman, someone from Jairus' household came and said: "Thy daughter is dead: why troublest thou the Master any further?" (Mark 5:35).

Honestly speaking, unless your loved one has died and you are trying to get him resurrected, your problem certainly isn't this bad, is it? I can imagine the utter hopelessness Jairus must have felt when he heard that his precious young daughter had died. He may have thought, *If we never would have stopped to heal that woman, my daughter would be alive.*

However, look at Jesus' reaction. Did He break down and start condemning Himself for not being on time to save the girl? No, He began to encourage this distraught father, "Jairus, I know this looks bad; but just keep hanging on to God's transforming power."

The only thing that matters is that God's Word works!

When we were in Amarillo, Texas, as assistant pastors, we were involved in prison ministry. Every Sunday afternoon we would go and preach in the prisons; Wally would minister to the men and I would minister to the women's side. One particular Sunday we had been invited out to dinner by one of the couples in the church. The woman was a new Christian who was just getting ahold of the Word, but her husband was not a Christian. Nevertheless, he had come to church with her that Sunday.

We accepted their invitation; however, we told them that we would have to leave right after dinner to fulfill our obligation to the prison. Then the woman asked if she and her husband could go with us and watch us minister. We thought it would be strange to have an unsaved person accompany us to a prison service, but the husband wanted to go so we said that it was fine with us.

The woman and I finished ministering first, and we were sitting in the waiting room waiting for Wally and her husband. She said to me, "Marilyn, I know my husband is going to get saved. The Bible says that if I believe on the Lord, my house will get saved." (Acts 16:31.) She had gotten ahold of God's Word—His transforming power. We had begun to speculate on the different ways that her husband's salvation might come about when the prison chaplain walked in and said, "I've got good news! Pastor Hickey just prayed with your husband, and he received the Lord."

Friend, it doesn't matter when, where, or how God's Word will begin to transform our situations, does it? The only thing that matters is that God's Word works!

What happened when they arrived at Jairus' house? This was such a sad occasion. Jairus' house was full of people, who were weeping and wailing over his daughter:

And when he [Jesus] was come in, he saith unto them, Why make ye this ado, and weep? the damsel is not dead, but sleepeth.

Mark 5:39

The people began to laugh at Jesus—they thought He was nuts—but it did not matter to Jesus what they thought. He just made everyone leave the room where the girl was lying, except for His three disciples, Jairus, and his wife:

And he took the damsel by the hand, and said unto her; Tali-tha cumi; which is, being interpreted, Damsel, I say unto thee, arise.

Mark 5:41

Jesus was saying, "Little lamb, it is getting up time." Doesn't that sound like Jesus? Isn't that just what He would say? I remember when my mother used to wake me up when I was little. She'd kiss me and say, "Honey, it's time to get up." That was just the warmest, sweetest feeling!

What did the young girl do when Jesus spoke the transforming power of God's Word into her spirit?

And straightway the damsel arose, and walked; for she was of the age of twelve years. And they were astonished with a great astonishment.

Mark 5:42

She got up and began to walk around. I can just picture the look of shock on the faces of all those people who had laughed at Jesus. They were probably stunned to silence!

Friend, put your faith in God's Word—Jesus. Although your children (or other loved ones) may be dead in trespasses, sins, and all kinds of garbage, you must not let go of God's transforming power. Whether they live at home with you or on the other side of the world, one day Jesus is going to say to them, "Little lamb, little lamb, it's time to rise up out of your sins." And do you know what those little lambs are going to do? That's right, they are going to get up too. So be sure to keep on Satan-proofing your loved ones, and refuse to let go of God's transforming power for their lives.

Just as Jesus told that girl to arise, God is saying to you that it is time for your children to arise out of the defeating lifestyles in which they may be functioning. It's time for them to be transformed into the wonderful vision that God has for them. Did you know that God has made a special promise to you fathers concerning your children:

> *And he shall turn the heart of the fathers to the children, and the heart of the children to their fathers, lest I come and smite the earth with a curse.*

> Malachi 4:6

Perhaps your relationship with your children has been strained lately, or maybe it is just plain "shot!" Be encouraged because this is a day of enlightenment. Your children aren't going down the drain—no matter what might have transpired in the past. From this day forward, we mothers and fathers are enlightened and we are going to learn how to deal with our children.

Consider: The Mother's Faith

We've been looking at the father's faith; now I want to look at the mother's faith. There is something very unique about a mother's faith. It allows us to give our children the benefit of the doubt despite how bad the situation may appear. We mothers seem to be equipped with some extra mercy concerning our children; so we can believe that, sooner or later, our children are going to come out on top of their circumstances.

The Syrophenician mother certainly stretched out in supernatural faith on behalf of her hurting daughter:

> *And, behold, a woman of Canaan came out of the same coasts, and cried unto him, saying, Have mercy on me, O Lord, thou son of David; my daughter is grievously vexed with a devil.*

> Matthew 15:22

This woman's daughter was demon-possessed. Your children may not be this troubled, but could they be influenced by what they watch on television?

Have you ever monitored the programs that your children like to watch? Do you know what kinds of values they are developing based upon the immoral lifestyles of those characters portrayed on television? Friend, become more involved with your children so that Satan doesn't pick them off like ducks at a shooting gallery. Your children are your fruit, so make sure they learn how to be valuable to themselves as well as to others.

Looking back on this desperate mother who sought Jesus' help, she said her daughter was grievously vexed. The spirits possessing this girl were hurting her, and she needed to be set free. The devil was hurting that poor girl then, and he is still hurting people today. Living a lifestyle beneath that which God has destined for people hurts! So the woman came to Jesus:

But he answered her not a word. And his disciples came and besought him, saying, Send her away; for she crieth after us. But he answered and said, I am not sent but unto the lost sheep of the house of Israel.

Matthew 15:23,24

I love this woman's tenacity. She could easily have been offended by Jesus and the disciples and walked away. But instead, she came closer and began to worship Jesus. She said, "Lord, help me":

But he answered and said, It is not meet to take the children's bread, and to cast it to dogs. And she said, Truth, Lord: yet the dogs eat of the crumbs which fall from their masters' table.

Matthew 15:26,27

Jesus actually called her a dog! But did she turn away and run home crying? No! She was determined to get ahold of Jesus Christ, the living Word—God's transforming power—for her daughter! She was not about to let anything stop her, and she got the victory for her daughter:

Then Jesus answered and said unto her, O woman, great is thy faith: be it unto thee even as thou wilt. And her daughter was made whole from that very hour.

Matthew 15:28

Offenses are deliberate traps that have been laid by the devil; and if you're not very careful, you'll fall into one of these traps and miss your miracle. Perhaps indignation would be the natural response to some situation, but it's your choice as to whether you are going to operate in the natural (your old nature) or the supernatural (your new nature). The woman Jesus was talking with chose not to become offended by the way Jesus treated her and by the rudeness of His disciples. She chose not to be offended, even when Jesus called her a dog. Rather, she humbled herself and said, "Lord, if I am a dog, I am Your dog and I want the crumbs that fall from Your table."

Years ago, a man with a marvelous, miracle ministry came to our church. He really led a consecrated life and fasted and prayed so much that he looked like a pile of bones. There were always so many miracles when he came, but there also were so many people who were offended by him. Our telephone at the church would ring off the wall with people saying, "He is so crude." And he was. I remember one night he said to a woman, "What are you doing up here tonight? I prayed for you last night. Sit down!" She just kind of crept off and sat down and missed her miracle. But do you know that the people who hung in there and refused to become offended experienced many miracles in their lives?

Now don't get me wrong; I am not saying that this man was right to be so offensive. I don't really know what his problem was, but I do know that the people who allowed his crude personality to cause them to become offended really missed out on their miracles.

Consider: Power to Transform the Past

The fourth thing I want you to understand is that God's transforming power can correct situations that may have resulted from improper parenting. Let's face it, no matter how good our intentions may be, sometimes we parents promote failure in our children rather than faith.

One day my son, Mike, said, "Mother, if you and Dad had put half as much into me as you put into Sarah, I would be much further down the road." I almost responded defensively, "Well, Michael, we tried. But you really botched it up sometimes, and we had a very hard time dealing with you."

But the Lord said to me, "Don't do that; don't be defensive at all; just admit where you blew it." So, instead of reading my son the riot act, I said, "Michael, you're right; there were things that we did wrong. Can you find it in your heart to forgive us?" He said, "Of course I do."

Perhaps you have made some mistakes raising your children. But is God going back on His Word (Proverbs 11:21) just because you may have blown it? No, because God's transforming power can undo any mistakes we may have made in raising our children. Although it was certainly unintentional, I failed my son in some areas; but I never failed to love him. And I know God is going to bring Michael through despite my mistakes.

There was a little boy born in Egypt who, if not for his mother's faith, would never have achieved God's goal for his life:

And the woman conceived, and bare a son: and when she saw him that he was a goodly child, she hid him three months.

Exodus 2:2

The Hebrew word for *goodly* can mean "beautiful, prosperous, and excellent"[1]; that's what this baby's mother saw when she looked into his tiny face. All babies are beautiful to their mothers, right? I've never heard a mother say, "I've got the ugliest baby in the world." Have you? The baby may have big ears or a big nose, and most newborns look kind of beat up. But to the mother, that baby is absolutely beautiful.

I don't blame Jochebed one bit for refusing to allow her son to be killed because of some stupid Egyptian law: "And Pharaoh charged all his people, saying, Every son that is born ye shall cast into the river, and every daughter ye shall save alive" (Exodus 1:22).

Jochebed really had a mother's faith for her baby. She hid him for three months; then she put him in an ark and floated him down a river full of crocodiles—the baby finally ended up in Pharaoh's daughter's bathtub. When Pharaoh's daughter drew the baby out of the Nile River, she had compassion on him. She named the baby Moses, which means "drawing out,"[2] took him home, and raised him as her own son.

Because of his mother's faith, Moses' life was spared; and he was highly educated and had the best of everything. After some really serious learning experiences, Moses, at 80 years of age, answered God's call upon his life to deliver the Israelites out of Egypt.

Looking back on the circumstances surrounding Moses' birth would you have foreseen all of this in his future? I doubt it, but God's transforming power turned Moses' life around. So, instead of being killed instantly at birth or becoming dinner for a bunch of hungry crocodiles, Moses became the deliverer of Israel.

...regardless of their beginnings, God has plans for your children.

When we compare Moses' situation to what we may be experiencing, we can say that not all Christian parents were born again at early ages. Some of us spent a lot of years living in sinful lifestyles; and therefore, our children were raised in ungodly homes—they may have had very difficult lives. But regardless of their beginnings, God has plans for your children—they may be future deliverers in the Body of Christ. So stop feeling guilty about mistakes you may have made in parenting your children. Seek God and repent. Then ask your children to forgive you, and stand on God's Word—His transforming power for their lives.

Consider: Catching the Faith Vision

The last thing I want you to consider is catching God's faith vision for your children. Oftentimes, we see reflections of ourselves and our spouses when we look at our children. And that's okay as long as the traits we see are in accord with God's will. However, what happens when we or our spouses have been involved in alcohol abuse, drug addiction, or other debilitating kinds of lifestyles? How about your children? Have you caught a glimpse of God's faith vision? Don't look at what is occurring in the natural; see your loved ones by faith!

I can remember when Mike used to come by the church while he was high on drugs. He was so pitiful. But one day God showed me how to catch His faith vision for my son. I would envision Mike with a Bible in his hands, praising the Lord just as God saw when He looked at my son. Then one summer night, I saw Mike standing in the back of the church with his hands lifted high in the air, and he was singing in tongues. Praise God! His faith vision had been manifested from the spiritual realm into the natural realm.

Friend, hold on to God's transforming power and begin to see what God sees when He looks at your loved ones. God never called believers to be conformers, right? We are here to be transformers so we can subdue the earth as He put us here to do in the first place.

I want you to know that I am praying for you to begin to take authority over your circumstances—that's what God has destined for all people:

So God created man in his own image, ...and God said unto them, Be fruitful, and multiply, and replenish the earth, and subdue it: ...

Genesis 1:27,28

God does not want your family to become another statistic in the "failure of the family" epidemic. If you will take the precautions I have been talking about for guarding yourself and your home against Satan's divisive elements, then your family will not give way to the force of his storms. By faith, I am standing with you in prayer. God has commissioned you to be a Satan-proofer; and from this day forward, the devil doesn't have a chance in your home!

CHAPTER 11

———»·o·«———

No Longer Bound

Mankind's deliverance from Satan's power is the reason Jesus went to the Cross. The Bible says, "If the Son therefore shall make you free, ye shall be free indeed" (John 8:36). Yet, many Christians who have accepted salvation are still very bound in their souls (mind, will, and emotions) although free in their spirits.

I am reminded of a story about some beautiful caged birds that had been held captive all of their lives. A man once saw them and pitied them because they were caged and not free. Thinking he would do them a favor, the man opened the cage for the birds to fly to freedom. Although he encouraged them to come out, the birds fluttered about in their cage, sticking close to its sides, refusing to leave the sanctity of their bondage and fly to freedom. And so it is with many Christians.

They have become so accustomed to their captivity that it is more comfortable for them to remain bound to their old habits and ways of thinking than to go free. (This hinders Satan-proofing; they may do spiritual warfare for their loved ones but have a hard time Satan-proofing themselves.)

Perhaps this hits close to where you or a neighbor or a loved one lives. Bondage is not of God, and I want to show you how you can loose the ties that bind you and walk free in Jesus' name!

The Bible points to three specific areas where you can come into bondage: 1) the flesh; 2) the soul, which is your mind, will, and emotions; and 3) the area of the demonic.

For example, suppose three different people were dealing with anger in some form or another. (You can substitute any problem for anger, such as fear, lust, greed, etc.) All three people deal with this problem using the Word, but only one gets the victory. God does not have any pets, so why does only one person receive the victory? Is it because there is something wrong with the other two? No. Just because all three people are struggling with anger doesn't mean they are all dealing with the same problem. Anger is the "symptom" of the problem, it is not the problem. So if one person received the victory and the other two didn't, then only one of them dealt with the root cause of their anger. The other two haven't been able to discern the root cause of their behavior.

It's just as if someone with a headache went to a doctor. The doctor diagnoses the problem as a tumor and treats it with radiation and chemotherapy. The real problem is not a tumor, but failing eyesight. Obviously, no matter how strong the treatments are, they won't cure the headache; only a new pair of glasses will help.

Perhaps this is what is happening to you or your loved one. You deal with things that you think are problems, but they are only symptoms. You need to become aware of the root of what is causing you to become angry, fearful, jealous, etc.

Area of the Flesh

In our trio of angry people, the first person's anger is caused by his flesh nature—he naturally gets angry. The way to know if something that you are dealing with is in your flesh is if it can be controlled by your will. You can deal with a problem of the flesh and receive the victory by crucifying your flesh:

I am crucified with Christ: nevertheless I live; yet not I, but Christ liveth in me: and the life which I now live in the flesh I live by the faith of the Son of God, who loved me, and gave himself for me.

Galatians 2:20

When you crucify your flesh, you are making a conscious decision to glorify Christ and are able to control your damaging actions or emotions. The first angry person in our trio was delivered of his anger using Scripture—he crucified his flesh. The other two people crucified their flesh, but nothing happened because they are dealing with anger that is not based in the flesh, but in other areas.

Area of the Soul

The anger of the person who is dealing with a wounded soul is not natural anger of the flesh. That person has a very painful, festering wound in his soul, which is the seat of the mind, will, and emotions. He can crucify his flesh all day long, but until he allows the Lord to deal with his wounded soul, he won't be delivered.

The way to recognize if you have a wounded soul is to determine if you have developed a pattern of reacting in the same way to stressful situations. A problem with your flesh nature will show in how you act; a wounded soul manifests itself in how you react. If you always react in a certain way before you have a chance to stop yourself, then you are dealing with a wounded soul.

If you had a wound on your physical body that you hadn't cleansed, it would become infected. If the infection was not dealt with in a timely fashion, it would carry the poison throughout your body. Likewise, if you are wounded in your emotions and do not cleanse your mind with the truth of the Word, then your mind will become infected with things that are poisonous to your soul, such as lies about yourself or others. If you don't deal with these lies, they will course through your thought processes. Pretty soon every thought will become infected with these lies.

Something that is infected hurts, and if someone bumps up against it, you wince. That wincing is a reaction. In the same way, if somebody bumps into your festering emotional wound, you react out of pain. You wince. You blow up in anger.

Suppose you failed miserably at something when you were seven years old. It wounded you because it was embarrassing and humiliating. This is where the infection began because you thought, *I failed so miserably at this because I'm pathetic*. Then you started seeing everything through the thought, *I'm pathetic*. This lie courses through your whole thought process, affecting everything you think about yourself and everything you do.

Festering Emotional Wounds

Let's pretend you are at a fashion show. This fashion show is quite unusual, however, because the models are modeling their wounded souls. Ms. Jealousy is our first model. She is modeling her, "Why not me?" wound. Her first response is always, "Why wasn't I chosen? Why didn't you invite me? Why didn't you call me?" The bacteria or lie that was taken into her soul at the time it was wounded and has consequently become a permanent part of her thought life is, *I'm not accepted*. Because she doesn't feel accepted, she's constantly striving for acceptance. She wants others to bring her into what she perceives as the "inner circle."

Our next model, Ms. Pride, is modeling her, "I'm better than you," wound. Basically what happens to Ms. Pride is she thinks that everything she possesses (experiences with the Lord, her car, etc.) is better than yours. The lie that infected Ms. Pride's wounded soul is, "I have to be the most important." Because she believes this lie, she can't vacate the throne long enough to allow God to be Lord over her life.

Ms. Shame is another example of a wounded soul. She is modeling her, "I don't want anyone to see me," wound. The bacteria or lie that is festering in her soul is that, *I'm not worth anything*. Although Ms. Shame agreed to model in this fashion show, she doesn't want anyone looking at her. She feels that no matter what she's doing, or what situation she is in, everyone (including you) is staring at her.

Ms. Fear is our next model. Because she constantly "freaks out," she is modeling her, "Freak out," wound. When confronted with a situation she doesn't know how to deal with, she panics and freaks out (a sudden burst of perspiration, a shortness of breath, a ringing in the ears, becomes paralyzed and can't think, has an urge to bolt from the room, etc). The lie that came in when Ms. Fear's soul was wounded is, *Nobody will protect me*.

The Bible says God is Ms. Fear's Protector, but she can't believe a lie and the truth at the same time. People who are in fear don't realize that this lie (or any of these lies that our models have bought into) is a stronghold in their minds, and they're living their lives according to it. They may mentally assent to the fact that they believe God can protect them, but the standard that they live by is, *Nobody will protect me.*

Ms. No Responsibility is now coming down the runway. You will notice that she is modeling her, "I didn't do it!" wound. Her normal response to everything is, "It's not my fault. Don't blame me." The bacteria that infected her soul and the lie that she believes is, *I can't face it.* At the time that the wounding took place, it was simply too big to face and she believes that if she faces it, the enormity of the event will destroy her because she will have to accept some responsibility or accountability for what happened.

The "shy, embarrassed" wound is being modeled by Ms. Giggles. We all know people like her who giggle regardless of the situation confronting them. At first, you may think Ms. Giggles is a happy-go-lucky person, but after you get to know her you realize she doesn't necessarily enjoy her giggling. It's an involuntary response. The words that come out of her mouth when she verbalizes anything are, "I can't believe I did that. I can't believe I said that." The lie or bacteria that infected her soul at the time of wounding is, *I'm so dumb.*

Ms. Anger is ready to explode. She is modeling her "frustration" wound. When she reacts in anger—it doesn't really matter what words come out of her mouth, it is the "force" with which they come at you. Ms. Anger's wound is there; it's ugly, pressurized, and she finally gives in to the temptation to vent it and it squirts all over the place. So when you bump into her anger by saying something quite normal, the poisonous stuff that spews forth from her mouth literally squirts all over you and leaves you with a feeling of *Yuck. What was that?*

Ms. Anger walks away remorseful, and thinks, *I can't believe I did that.* She finds it hard to apologize because her angry reaction was way out of proportion to whatever was going on in the first place. She would rather pretend the incident never happened.

The lie that Ms. Anger accepted into her soul is, *I can't forgive"* She does not realize that her unforgiveness will turn into bitterness and cause what comes out of her mouth to be poisonous to both her and her poor innocent victim(s).

Our next model is Ms. Invisible, who is modeling her "nobody cares about me," wound. She feels like there is nothing she could ever do to make people acknowledge her presence. Whenever she is in a group and is saying something, someone else will probably blurt in and start talking right over her and no one will even notice. She constantly feels like nothing she says is quite funny or appropriate enough. She will always feel like she is only a part of the woodwork. The lie that Ms. Invisible believes is that *No one will ever care about me*, because she feels her experiences have taught her this.

You can recognize if your soul has been wounded by both your verbal or non-verbal reactions.

Ms. Control is modeling her "It always has to be my way," wound. She always has a better way to do everything. The lie that infected her soul is, *"I can't trust anybody.*

"Who cares?" is the wound Ms. Bad Attitude is modeling. Her common complaints include, "What does this have to do with anything, anyway? What does this have to do with me, anyway? I can't believe how stupid this is!" The bacteria that infected Ms. Bad Attitude's soul is, *I don't need anybody.* She believes she is completely self-sufficient, which is a lie because we all need God and each other. Because Ms. Bad Attitude can't meet her own needs, she is pretty unhappy, but she would never acknowledge her unhappiness.

Ms. People Pleaser is our final model. She is modeling her "need to please you" wound. She has such an inordinate need to just please, she wearies the people who are around her because she is constantly seeking their reassurance: "Do I look okay? Is this what you want? Is this what you want me to do? Is this what you want me to say? Well, do you think we should put this over here?" The lie that infected her soul is, *I'm not acceptable.*

These are only some examples of a wounded soul. You can recognize if your soul has been wounded by both your verbal or non-verbal reactions. Matthew 12:34 says, "For out of the abundance of the heart the mouth speaketh." So you truly know what's coming out of your heart when you "react" before you have the opportunity to think. Your "reaction" comes directly from your heart before your brain has time to digest what is going on.

Effects of Traumatic Events

If something traumatic happened to you when you were a child, it could have caused any number of different emotions—fear, pain, anger. Your traumatic event could have been the death of a loved one, molestation, or divorce. Regardless of the event, if you were traumatized by it, it wounded your soulish man and caused an infection to set in.

For example, a young man's father was killed when he was only four years old. As an adult, this man may not realize he is carrying animosity toward God in his heart. And perhaps at the time of his father's death some well-meaning adult told him God took his father to be with Him. The son's response to God was, "Thank You a lot, God. You have all those angels and I only had one daddy. You needed my daddy, too?" Without even realizing it, this man subconsciously refuses to forgive God for taking his father, and his unforgiveness will remain subconscious until it's revealed by the Holy Spirit. He needs the Holy Spirit to reveal what the wound is and the lie or infection that was taken into his heart at the time of its wounding.

The wound itself—the instance when he was hurt—is not the problem. No one could help him with the initial wound because it is already healed and scarred over. He can't go back to when he was four years old and correct that wrong. What is destroying this man now and what has to be healed is the infection he has carried with him since he was four.

If there is an infected wound that has you in bondage to a sinful attitude or action, then you need to allow the Holy Spirit to deal with it. You don't have to revisit every single thing that ever happened to you, just the ones in which "bacteria" came into your system through a lie.

The infection must be lanced, and the only tool you can use to "cut" an emotional wound is the Word:

> *For the Word of God is quick, and powerful, and sharper than any twoedged sword, piercing even to the dividing asunder of soul and spirit....*
>
> Hebrews 4:12

To lance the wound you must first recognize that you have a problem that did not die when you crucified your flesh. Then you must want God to heal you of this hurt. This hunger will lead you to prayer. In prayer, you must ask the Holy Spirit to show you the area of your soul that needs healing.

When He reveals the point in your life where the wound took place and the lie of the devil came in, ask Him to give you a Scripture that will counter the lie you've agreed with for all these years. For example, if the lie is that "no one will ever protect you," the Scripture you can stand on is God's promise to never leave you, nor forsake you (see Hebrews 13:5). Then repent for believing the devil's lie. This will pull down Satan's strongholds in your life and the vain imaginations in your mind.

Once the Holy Spirit gives you a Scripture to stand on, verbally embrace and confess what God's Word says about you instead of the devil's lie. Ask God by the power of the Holy Spirit to quicken you when you are habitually getting ready to "react" according to the lie you believed, and to help you respond to God's truth instead. Confide in a trusted friend in this healing process and ask them to assist you by holding you accountable when you are in the midst of a pressurized situation. They can gently but firmly remind you, "That's how you would have reacted in the past before you learned the truth about yourself."

Then ask God to supernaturally touch and heal the wound. Choose to step out of the prison that the wound has caused in your life and forgive the person(s) who caused or contributed to your soul getting wounded. The way to know if the healing process is complete is when the memory of the wound brings forth no more pain and when the way you used to react under pressure ceases or falls away like a scab falls away when a wound in the natural is healed.

Let the Holy Spirit deal with you. If you don't allow Him to supernaturally heal you, then your wound will continue to fester in your soul, leaving you vulnerable to demonic activity. As you continue reacting to the pain in your soul, demonic spirits of fear, anger, etc., can begin to move in on you. Then, the next time you react, you've opened the door for them to come against you. When that happens, your problem will go to a whole new level—they will begin to pressure you to do things you don't want to do.

Area of the Demonic

Anger that is out of control is what the third person in our trio of angry people is dealing with. This man is a normal-functioning, regular Christian who is oppressed by demons! The only way this man can be delivered of his bondage of anger is to "cast out" his demons just as Jesus "cast out" the thieves from the Temple:

> *...Jesus went into the temple, and began to cast out them that sold and bought in the temple, and overthrew the tables of the moneychangers, and the seats of them that sold doves; And he taught, saying unto them, Is it not written, My house shall be called of all nations the house of prayer? but ye have made it a den of thieves.*

Mark 11:15,17

God called you His Temple (1 Corinthians 3:16); and He gave you a description of this Temple in the Old Testament. The entrance to the Temple was the outer court, which was accessible to anyone. Next was the inner court, which was restricted only to the Jews. Finally was the Holy of Holies, where God dwelt and where only the High Priest could enter.

Likewise, your body is the outer court of your physical Temple—it is accessible to anyone who talks to you, shakes your hand, or greets you on the street. Your soul (which is the seat of your mind, will, and emotions) is your inner court—you are more picky about who you allow into your heart as friends, mentors, and teachers. Your spirit is the Holy of Holies where God Himself resides—only Jesus, your Great High Priest, and the Holy Spirit have access into your spirit.

Just as the physical Temple in Mark 11 is a symbol of your spirit, the thieves in this account are symbols of demons because demons do the work of the devil, who comes to steal from you (John 10:10). Jesus didn't go into the Holy of Holies to cast out the thieves; He cleansed the courtyards. The same thing happens when someone is delivered from demonic oppression—the "thieves" are cast out! In fact, when the Bible said Jesus cast out the thieves, the Greek word *ekballo*[1] is used for that phrase; this Greek word is the same one used for the phrase when He cast out demons.

So in the same vein, when dealing with demonic oppression in Christians, you don't cast them out of the person's spirit because the spirit is clean, pure, holy, and the residence of God Himself! You cast them out of the person's body and soul, the Temple's courtyards.

Identifying the source of the problem is the most important step. Once you've identified your problem area, be it the flesh, a wounded soul, or demonic oppression, you can break the demonic ties that bind you and/or your loved ones. You'll discover that the Word of God is true. That if Jesus has set you free, no demon in hell can bind you, nor can the gates of hell prevail against you. Jesus is Lord!

Stay Free

If you have been involved in sin or allowed the devil to affect your life in any way, the most important thing you can remember is Christ does not condemn you: "For God sent not his Son into the world to condemn the world; but that the world through him might be saved" (John 3:17).

God's Word says everyone has sinned and fallen short of His glory (Romans 3:23), so you are not unique if you have made mistakes. The fact that you have sinned and, even unknowingly, allowed the devil access into your heart has made you an ideal candidate for Christ's saving power:

> *For when we were yet without strength, in due time Christ died for the ungodly. But God commendeth his love toward us, in that, while we were yet sinners, Christ died for us.*
>
> Romans 5:6,8

In fact, there are three power keys that God has given you to deliver you and set you free.

Repentance

The first thing you need to do in order to receive deliverance is to repent. The Lord is calling for you to reach out to Him in remorse for your actions and attitudes:

> *...They that are whole have no need of the physician, but they that are sick: I came not to call the righteous, but sinners to repentance.*
>
> Mark 2:17

154

God doesn't call you to repent because He is angry or frustrated; it is the "goodness of God" that leads you to repentance (Romans 2:4).

In Paul's first letter to the church at Corinth, he called for the purification of the church's sins. The people read his letter and, in their sorrow, turned to God and repented. Paul explained in his second letter that the sorrow they felt was something to be excited about:

> *Now I rejoice not that ye were made sorry, but that ye sorrowed to repentance: for ye were made sorry after a godly manner, ...For godly sorrow worketh repentance to salvation not to be repented of: but the sorrow of the world worketh death.*
>
> 2 Corinthians 7:9,10

Repentance brings a change in your life because it is a serious, sincere, heartfelt action.

You too should feel a godly sorrow for your attitudes and actions—a sinful lifestyle, laziness in your walk with God, a bitter spirit—so you can repent to God.

Repentance brings a change in your life because it is a serious, sincere, heartfelt action. The Greek word for *repent* is *metanoeo*, which means "to think differently." God wants you to change your life by changing your attitude:

> *...Turn ye even to me with all your heart, and with fasting, and with weeping, and with mourning: And rend your heart, and not your garments, and turn unto the LORD your God: for he is gracious and merciful, slow to anger, and of great kindness and repenteth him of the evil.*
>
> Joel 2:12,13

Repentance is a physical as well as mental and spiritual activity. You need to fast, pray, and mourn (be sincerely sorry) for the pain you have caused your Father. Rededicate your life to Him and commit yourself to living a life that will glorify God.

Forgiveness

As soon as you repent, ask the Lord for forgiveness. Ask Him to search your heart for any impurity and to cast any uncleanness away from you.

Wash yourself in the blood of Jesus, which will make you whiter than snow (Psalms 51:7).

You may say, "God can't possibly forgive the things I have done. I have cheated on my spouse; neglected my children; taken drugs; worshiped the devil; and I lie, cheat, and steal. I am beyond God's forgiveness!" You are wrong. God said He is faithful and just to forgive *all* your sins and cleanse you of *all* unrighteousness (1 John 1:9). Remember, Christ didn't die on the cross for people who never committed an offense—He came to save chronic sinners!

> *Who hath delivered us from the power of darkness, and hath translated us into the kingdom of his dear Son: In whom we have redemption through his blood, even the forgiveness of sins.*
>
> Colossians 1:13,14

Learn to accept the simplicity and fullness of Christ's forgiveness. All you have to do to receive it is ask, with a repentant heart, to be cleansed: "And the prayer of faith shall save the sick, ...and if he have committed sins, they shall be forgiven him" (James 5:15).

Deliverance

With a cleansed heart and mind, you can now experience the fullness of your deliverance. Deliverance is not just for non-Christians who are possessed in their spirits by demons, but for Christians who are oppressed by demons in their bodies and souls.

If you have repented and asked for forgiveness but are still not free, you are not alone. Many of God's people are discouraged, in despair, hardened in their hearts, angry, frustrated, and puzzled because they don't know how to truly be set free from their bondages. Why? Because God's people "are destroyed for lack of knowledge:..." (Hosea 4:6).

There is nothing wrong with you! You aren't a bad Christian. You are experiencing difficulty in your spiritual walk because you don't know where your problem lies or how to be delivered from it.

The original Hebrew word that "knowledge" comes from is the root word *yada*. This word means "to know,"[2] but in a fuller sense it means "to become aware of or have the fullness of understanding." So it is not so much that you don't know God's Word— you've read it and studied it—but you need a fuller understanding of what you have read and studied.

Your understanding lies in Jesus, who said, "If ye continue in my word, ... ye shall know the truth, and the truth shall make you free" (John 8:31-32). Read God's Word and meditate on it. Ask Him to open your heart to understand it. And when you receive that fullness of revelation of the Word, then you will be set free!

If you believe demons are attacking you, I encourage you to seek the help of a sympathetic pastor who has a ministry steeped in the Word. Have people pray for you don't try to do it on your own. Although you have full authority over the devil and his demons, when you are demon oppressed, you are already dealing with serious deception and may lose your way in the process of deliverance. Surround yourself with Christians who will pray when you are not able.

If you are helping someone to be delivered, there are certain things you must remember. First of all, you have full authority over Satan and his devils and demons (Genesis 1:26; Psalms 8:5-8; Luke 10:19). Second, be watchful and sober (1 Peter 5:8-9). Third, submit yourself to God and resist the devil (James 4:7). Fourth, repent of any sin in your life.

When you move in the power of the Holy Spirit, you will have signs and wonders following after you, including the deliverance of demon-oppressed people:

And by the hands of the apostles were many signs and wonders wrought among the people. ...There came also a multitude out of the cities round about Jerusalem, bringing sick folks, and them which were vexed with unclean spirits: and they were healed every one.

Acts 5:12,16

When you are dealing with demons, you aren't fighting against the person who is oppressed; you are fighting a supernatural, spiritual battle. Therefore, you should be spiritually prepared.

For we wrestle not against flesh and blood, but against principalities, against powers, against the rulers of the darkness of this world, against spiritual wickedness in high places. Wherefore take unto you the whole armour of God, that ye may be able to withstand in the evil day, and having done all, to stand.

Ephesians 6:12,13

When you are saved, delivered, and/or set free from bondage of any kind, immediately get involved in Bible studies, learn how to pray, and share the news of your deliverance with the world. This holds true for anyone you've been praying for; encourage them to do the same.

Satan has declared war on the children of God; that includes you and those you love and care about. Right now you may feel as though the devil is winning. The truth is, he knows your weaknesses and will try to take every advantage he can to defeat you. He will try to steal your peace of mind, the love of your family and friends, the fellowship of Christians, and whatever else he can rob you of...even your life.

However, remember that you are armed with the love of God and the knowledge of His Word. When you understand the devil and his demons that attack you, and finally get hold of the authority you have in Christ, you will no longer be defenseless against the enemy. You will receive the victory you are promised by God.

You never have to lose another battle with the devil! And neither do your loved ones. Take hold of God's promises. Speak the Word to God, to yourself, and to the devil—and become a champion.

CHAPTER 12

Lifestyle of the Blessed and Victorious

This is just the beginning—you must now begin to apply what you've learned in these pages and keep your life cleansed of evil in order to live in freedom and victory.

Remember, you mustn't let your heart be filled with anger or frustration, fear or bitterness. You must fill your heart with God's Word, love, and joy. How can you do this? By making God a part of your lifestyle.

Someone told me that it takes 21 days for an action to become a habit, and six months for that habit to become a lifestyle. So, if God is not already a part of your lifestyle, for the next 21 days I want you to make an appointment with Him to pray, read your Bible, and meditate on the Scriptures that will help you through your day. Then, practice your authority over the devil by pleading the blood of Jesus over situations, speaking the Word whenever things start going awry, and setting all fears and temptations aside.

After your three weeks are over, you will have a habit that will bless you and keep you on track with God. Continue seeking God; in six months you will find your whole lifestyle has changed and you will experience the manifestations of God's victory in many areas of your life.

Strategy for Success

As a Christian, you must choose between allowing God and His angels to minister and help you, or letting Satan and his angels harass, tempt, and cause you (or your loved ones) to stumble in your faith. In this book I've revealed to you the key to choosing between winning or losing in spiritual warfare—which is knowing the Word of God—and the ten pieces of strategic advice the Word has for you to get free and live free. Let's look at them again:

1.) Put on the whole armor of God:

> *Finally, my brethren, be strong in the Lord, and in the power of his might. Put on the whole armour of God, that ye may be able to stand against the wiles of the devil. Stand therefore, having your loins girt about with truth, and having on the breastplate of righteousness; And your feet shod with the preparation of the gospel of peace; Above all, taking the shield of faith, wherewith ye shall be able to quench all the fiery darts of the wicked. And take the helmet of salvation, and the sword of the Spirit, which is the word of God.*
>
> Ephesians 6:10,11,14-17

Nothing the devil throws at you can penetrate this spiritual armor, which is made up of God's truth, righteousness, peace, faith, salvation, and Word. You receive God's truth and righteousness through your Savior, Jesus Christ (John 1:17; 1 Corinthians 1:30). Peace and faith are fruit of the Spirit (Galatians 5:22); and salvation is the gift of God (John 3:16). Finally, God's Word is given to you in the form of the Bible, the Holy Spirit, and Jesus Christ (John 1:1).

Satan and his army cannot penetrate God's holy hedge of protection, so surround yourself with these blessed gifts of the Father every day.

2.) Know Satan's devices:

> *Lest Satan should get an advantage of us: for we are not ignorant of his devices.*
>
> 2 Corinthians 2:11

3.) Don't allow anger, resentment, or unforgiveness in your life because that allows the devil to come in and take over:

> *Wherefore putting away lying, …Be ye angry, and sin not: let not the sun go down upon your wrath: Neither give place to the devil.*

Ephesians 4:25-27

4.) Yield to God's commandments and will for your life; and fight against the devil's temptations:

> *Submit yourselves therefore to God. Resist the devil, and he will flee from you. Draw nigh to God, and he will draw nigh to you….*

James 4:7,8

5.) Be realistic, earnest, and watchful about the things you allow into your life (and your loved ones' lives when possible), such as attitudes, entertainment, and relationships:

> *Be sober, be vigilant; because your adversary the devil, as a roaring lion, walketh about, seeking whom he may devour.*

1 Peter 5:8

6.) Overcome the devil by the blood of Jesus:

> *And they overcame him by the blood of the Lamb, and by the word of their testimony; and they loved not their lives unto the death.*

Revelation 12:11

7.) Overcome the devil by the Word:

> *I have written unto you, fathers, because ye have known him that is from the beginning. I have written unto you, young men, because ye are strong, and the word of God abideth in you, and ye have overcome the wicked one.*

1 John 2:14

8.) Overcome addictions and bondages by the power of the Holy Spirit:

For as many as are led by the Spirit of God, they are the sons of God. For ye have not received the spirit of bondage again to fear; but ye have received the Spirit of adoption, whereby we cry, Abba, Father.

Romans 8:14,15

9.) Overcome the temptations and pains of the world by faith:

For whatsoever is born of God overcometh the world: and this is the victory that overcometh the world, even our faith.

1 John 5:4

10.) Overcome the devil by reminding him that he is ultimately and utterly defeated:

And the devil that deceived them was cast into the lake of fire and brimstone where the beast and the false prophet are, and shall be tormented day and night forever and ever.

Revelation 20:10

If you have been bound by sin, obsessed by damaging emotions, or even oppressed by unclean spirits, there is no condemnation for you if you accept Jesus' salvation and deliverance. However, if God is convicting you to cleanse your life of Satan's influences, I encourage you to prayerfully begin that process today. Begin with the ten steps listed above.

Word-based Attitudes

When I studied the Sermon on the Mount, I realized that Jesus was not only telling us whom God would bless, but He was also giving us the attitudes that we should exhibit as Christians:

Blessed are the poor in spirit [humble]: *for their's is the kingdom of heaven. Blessed are they that mourn* [repentant]: *for they shall be comforted. Blessed are the meek: for they shall inherit the earth. Blessed are they which do hunger and thirst after righteousness: for they shall be filled. Blessed are the merciful: for they shall obtain mercy. Blessed are the pure in heart: for they shall see God. Blessed are the peacemakers: for they shall be called the children of God. Blessed are they which are persecuted for righteousness' sake: for their's is the kingdom of heaven. Blessed are ye, when men shall revile you, and persecute you, and shall say all manner of evil against you falsely, for my sake. Rejoice, and be exceeding glad: for great is your reward in heaven: for so persecuted they the prophets which were before you.*

Matthew 5:3-12

Jesus called us to be humble, repentant, meek, desirous of spiritual things, merciful, pure in heart, peaceful, willing to be persecuted for Christ's sake, and prepared to praise and rejoice in God. When you begin to bring your life in line with God's Word in these areas, God's promises will be made manifest in your life.

> *When you begin to bring your life in line with God's Word in these areas, God's promises will be made manifest in your life.*

Prayer and Fasting

Prayer is such an important part of your day. I encourage you to begin your day with a cleansing prayer in which you ask the Holy Spirit to search out any sin or bad attitudes that are in your heart. Repent of those things and plead the blood of Jesus over your mind, will, and emotions. (Remember to plead the blood over your loved ones too.)

Don't pray the same thing over and over again, and certainly don't make your prayers something with which you try to impress people. Go to God secretly and in humbleness. Don't keep anything back—pour out your heart and your desires to Him—because He already knows everything inside you. There are no secrets with God, which I find comforting because He loves me and does everything He can to help me even though He knows all my secret sins and thoughts (Matthew 6:5-8).

Use the Lord's Prayer as your guide: "...Our Father which art in heaven, Hallowed be thy name. Thy kingdom come, Thy will be done in earth, as it is in heaven. Give us this day our daily bread. And forgive us our debt, as we forgive our debtors. And lead us not into temptation, but deliver us from evil: For thine is the kingdom, and the power, and the glory, forever. Amen" (Matthew 6:9-13).

Pray for your family and loved ones. Prayer for their specific needs is a general prayer in which you ask for God's protection and peace for that person. I like to pray Psalm 23 for my family members. I simply insert the name of the person I am praying for whenever the word "I" appears. For instance, when I pray for my husband I say:

The Lord is [Wally's] shepherd; [he] shall not want. He maketh [Wally] to lie down in green pastures: he leadeth [Wally] beside the still waters. He restoreth [his] soul: he leadeth [Wally] in the paths of righteousness for his name's sake. Yea, though [Wally] walks through the valley of the shadow of death, [he] will fear no evil: for thou art with [him]; thy rod and thy staff they comfort [him]. Thou preparest a table before [Wally] in the presence of [his] enemies: thou anointest [his] head with oil; [Wally's] cup runneth over. Surely goodness and mercy shall follow [Wally] all the days of [his] life: and [he] will dwell in the house of the LORD for ever.

When you pray, God wants you to ask for the things you want and need (as long as they are according to the Word): "...Ask, and it shall be given you; seek, and ye shall find; knock, and it shall be opened unto you. For every one that asketh receiveth; and he that seeketh findeth; and to him that knocketh it shall be opened" (Luke 11:9-10).

You also need to add to your daily prayers special times of fasting. You don't need to fast 40 days or even 24 hours; you can fast and pray to God for one meal out of the week, or you can go on an extended fast if there is a particular problem that you or a loved one is facing.

Jesus said that when you fast you should do it secretly. "Anoint your head and wash your face," giving the appearance of normality. (Matthew 6:16-18 NKJV.)

Lifestyle of Victory

Remember, you have the authority to trample on serpents and scorpions, devils and demons, and Satan (see Luke 10:19). Therefore, you have received a tremendous victory through Christ Jesus. It's time Christians started to live a lifestyle of victory.

Part of that lifestyle is to stop being afraid of the world, the future, Satan, or death: "For God hath not given us the spirit of fear; but of power, and of love, and of a sound mind" (2 Timothy 1:7). Jesus said that God will protect you and care for you:

Take no thought for your life, what ye shall eat, or what ye shall drink; nor yet for your body, what ye shall put on. Is not the life more than meat, and the body than raiment? Behold the fowls of the air: for they sow not, neither do they reap, nor gather into barns; yet your heavenly Father feedeth them. Are ye not much better than they? ...Consider the lilies of the field, how they grow; they toil not, neither do they spin: And yet I say unto you, That even Solomon in all his glory was not arrayed like one of these ...for your heavenly Father knoweth that ye have need of all these things. But seek ye first the kingdom of God, and his righteousness; and all these things shall be added unto you. Take therefore no thought for the morrow: for the morrow shall take thought for the things of itself ....

Matthew 6:25,26,28,29,32-34

The devil likes to attack you, but his arrows are more like boomerangs because God turns them around and imbeds them into the devil's own heart. You see, God turns every one of the devil's attacks into opportunities for blessings:

And we know that all things work together for good to them that love God, to them who are the called according to his purpose.

Romans 8:28

Jesus told His disciples that when He ascended into heaven, the Holy Spirit would come to them as the Comforter. (See John 16:7.) He sends that Spirit to you, filling you with power and truth: "But ye shall receive power, after that the Holy Ghost is come upon you..." (Acts 1:8).

Howbeit when he, the Spirit of truth, is come, he will guide you into all truth....

John 16:13

165

When you learn about the power and kingdom authority you have through Christ Jesus, and your responsibility to keep your life cleansed of Satan's influence, you will be set free from the bondages of the devil.

I won't tell you the battle is always easy—Satan will try to hit you at every angle. But through the power of God and the weapons of our warfare, winning over the enemy can become a lifestyle!

Lifetime Guarantee

The most important thing you can remember about living a life of liberty and victory in Jesus is that you can do all things through Him (Philippians 4:13). He will help make your dreams come true and fulfill the desires of your heart:

> *Delight thyself also in the LORD; and he shall give thee the desires of thine heart.*

> Psalms 37:4

Stand up to the devil—he is afraid of you and your God-given powers. Whenever you feel him coming against you, plead the blood of Jesus, speak the Word, and don't fear for your life (Revelation 12:11). If he takes or destroys anything that belongs to you (such as property or loved ones), tell him he has to repay you sevenfold (Proverbs 6:31).

You are guaranteed a life that is free of addictions, obsessions, bondages, and oppression. By living your life for God, and putting into action what you've learned in this book, you will receive a life of eternal peace, joy, love, abundance, and victory over Satan and deliverance from all of his demonic cohorts!

———————

101 Ways to Defeat the Devil

The three most important steps you can take to defeat the devil are:

1. Know that God has already won the battle over Satan. "And having spoiled principalities and powers, he made a shew of them openly, triumphing over them in it" (Colossians 2:15).

2. Realize that Jesus has given you power over the devil and his demons. "...upon this rock I will build my church; and the gates of hell shall not prevail against it" (Matthew 16:18).

3. Praise God for the victory He has arranged in advance for His people. "And I saw... them that had gotten the victory over the beast, and over his image, and over his mark, and over the number of his name...." (Revelation 15:2).

Learn to recognize the character of the devil, and use the weapons God has formed against him; Avoid devilish traps. Let God show you how to deal with every evil trait.

4. The devil is proud (Jeremiah 49:16). Defeat his pride by rejoicing in Jesus' triumph over him! Second Corinthians 2:14 says, "Now thanks be unto God, which always causeth us to triumph in Christ,..."

5. The devil is powerful (Ephesians 2:2). Confess God's authority over the devil and his demons! Luke 4:36 says, "...with authority and power he commandeth the unclean spirits, and they come out."

6. The devil is wicked (Matthew 13:38,39). Remember that Jesus has obtained everlasting victory over wickedness. Revelation 3:21 says, "To him that overcometh will I grant to sit with me in my throne, even as I also overcame...."

7. The devil intends evil in all his ways (Isaiah 59:7). Realize that God is the maker of good things. James 1:17 says, "Every good gift and every perfect gift is from above, and cometh down from the Father of lights...."

8. The devil is subtle (Genesis 3:1). Outsmart him by developing a firm foundation of Scripture. Colossians 1:23 says, "...continue in the faith grounded and settled, and be not moved away from the hope of the gospel...."

9. The devil is deceitful (Psalms 36:3-4). Use God's truth to overturn his lies. John 8:32 says, "And ye shall know the truth, and the truth shall make you free."

10. The devil is fierce (Revelation 13:2). Realize God has compassion on His people. Second Chronicles 30:9 says, "...your children shall find compassion... for the LORD your God is gracious and merciful, ...if ye return unto him."

11. The devil is a murderer (John 8:44). Remember, God is the creator and giver of life. John 1:3-4 says, "All things were made by him; ... In him was life; and the life was the light of men."

12. The devil is a destroyer (Psalms 119:95). Recognize the mighty power of God to restore. Joel 2:25 says, "And I will restore to you the years that the locust hath eaten...."

13. The devil is the accuser. (Revelation 12:10.) Go to Jesus as your Advocate before the Father. First John 2:1 says, "...And if any man sin, we have an advocate with the Father, Jesus Christ the righteous...."

14. The devil is a seducer. (1 Timothy 4:1.) Praise God that His anointing strengthens you to stand against temptation. First Corinthians 10:13 says, "...God is faithful, who...will with the temptation also make a way to escape...."

15. The devil is an oppressor. (Luke 13:16.) Use the power of the Holy Spirit, as Jesus did, to throw off the devil's oppression. Acts 10:38 says, "How God anointed Jesus of Nazareth with the Holy Ghost and with power...."

16. The devil is king over the demons. (Revelation 9:11.) Operate in the power of God's grace to be greater than the demonic realm. Exodus 18:11 says, "Now I know that the LORD is greater than all gods...."

Learn the game plan of the devil and oppose it! The devil has perfected his techniques over the years. He hopes to defeat you by keeping you ignorant of how he works. Become aware of his "game plan" and you can win every time!

17. He masquerades as good. (2 Corinthians 11:14.) Be cautious. 1 John 4:1 says, "Beloved, believe not every spirit, but try the spirits whether they are of God...."

18. The devil works false wonders. (2 Thessalonians 2:9.) Believe only the Word of God. First John 2:24, "...continue in the Son, and in the Father."

19. He tries to hinder God's people (Daniel 10:11-13)—Keep focused. Philippians 3:14 says, "I press toward the mark for the prize of the high calling of God in Christ Jesus."

20. The devil makes war on Christians. (Revelation 12:17.) Take up God's spiritual weapons. Second Corinthians 10:4 says, "(For the weapons of our warfare are not carnal, but mighty through God to the pulling down of strong holds;)..."

21. He opposes God's work. (Zechariah 3:1) —Be strong. Deuteronomy 31:6 says, "Be strong and of a good courage, fear not, nor be afraid of them: for the LORD thy God, he it is that doth go with thee; he will not fail thee, nor forsake thee."

22. Satan blinds the world to the truth of the gospel. (2 Corinthians 4:4.) Keep your eyes open. Matthew 13:16 says, "But blessed are your eyes, for they see...."

23. He causes sickness and disease. (Matthew 4:24.) Use God's Word to strengthen your body. Psalms 107:20 says, "He sent his word, and healed them...."

24. Satan is the father of lies. (2 Chronicles 18:20-21)—Learn the truth. Psalms 86:11 says, "Teach me thy way, O LORD; I will walk in thy truth...."

25. He tries to snare you. (1 Timothy 3:7) —Be wary. Romans 16:19 says, "...I would have you wise unto that which is good, and simple concerning evil."

26. He causes you to be troubled. (1 Samuel 16:14.) Put on the peace of God. Psalms 55:18 says, "He hath delivered my soul in peace from the battle that was against me: for there were many with me."

27. He steals, kills, and destroys. (John 10:10) —Be alert. Nahum 2:1 says, "...keep the munition, watch the way, make thy loins strong, fortify thy power mightily."

28. He tries to pervert Scriptures. (Acts 13:10.) Be strong in the Word. Psalm 119:110 says, "The wicked have laid a snare for me: yet I erred not from thy precepts."

29. Evil will increase in the last days. (2 Timothy 3:1-5,13.) Heed the signs of the times. Revelation 12:12, "...the devil is come down unto you, having great wrath, because he knoweth that he hath but a short time."

Realize that the devil's power is limited. Satan persuades people to look to him and turn from God. God has curbed Satan's power. Perverseness is overturned by God's almighty power.

30. Know that the devil cannot resist the power of the name of Jesus. Luke 10:17 says, "...Lord, even the devils are subject unto us through thy name."

31. Realize that the devil must obey Jesus Christ. Mark 1:27 says, "...for with authority commandeth he even the unclean spirits, and they do obey him."

32. Believe that Jesus gives you the power to command demons to go—and they have to obey. Mark 16:17 says, "...In my name shall they cast out devils...."

33. Exercise your power to silence the devil. Mark 1:34 says, "And he...cast out many devils; and suffered not the devils to speak, because they knew him."

Avoid the work of the devil. When you are born again, a new nature is born into your spirit. Your old nature often doesn't want to let go of past habits and thoughts and speech. God's Word will help you triumph over old ways.

34. Don't sin when you are angry. Ephesians 4:26-27 says, "Be ye angry, and sin not: let not the sun go down upon your wrath: Neither give place to the devil."

35. Avoid illegal drugs and alcohol. Ephesians 5:18 says, "And be not drunk with wine, wherein is excess; but be filled with the Spirit...."

36. Avoid bitterness. Ephesians 4:31 says, "Let all bitterness, and wrath, and anger, and clamour, and evil speaking, be put away from you, with all malice...."

37. Avoid the works of the flesh. Ephesians 5:11 says, "And have no fellowship with the unfruitful works of darkness, but rather reprove them."

38. Avoid the occult. Deuteronomy 18:10 says, "There shall not be found among you any one that maketh his son or his daughter to pass through the fire, or that useth divination, or an observer of times, or an enchanter, or a witch...."

39. Avoid other people who sin. 1 Corinthians 5:9-11 says, "...I have written unto you not to keep company, if any man that is called a brother be a fornicator, or covetous, or an idolater, or a railer, or a drunkard, or an extortioner...."

40. Avoid strife. Romans 16:17 says, "...mark them which cause divisions and offences contrary to the doctrine which ye have learned; and avoid them."

Believe that the battle is the Lord's. The devil's real battle is with God. When you accepted Jesus Christ, you became a soldier in God's army. You train at the hands of the greatest General ever! The Lord leads as you fight the enemy.

41. Don't be afraid. You're not alone it's God's battle! Second Chronicles 20:15,17 says, "...Be not afraid nor dismayed by reason of this great multitude; for the battle is not yours, but God's.... Ye shall not need to fight in this battle...."

42. Let God train you in righteous warfare. Psalms 144:1 says, "Blessed be the LORD my strength, which teacheth my hands to war, and my fingers to fight."

43. Ask God to cause you to triumph in every battle. Psalm 25:2 says, "O my God, I trust in thee: let me not be ashamed, let not mine enemies triumph over me."

44. Be confident in God's power. Psalms 27:3 says, "Though an host should encamp against me, my heart shall not fear...."

45. Don't fight alone, fight through God! Psalm 108:13 says, "Through God we shall do valiantly: for he it is that shall tread down our enemies."

46. Use God's strength—you are the work of His hands. Psalms 18:39 says, "For thou hast girded me with strength unto the battle...."

47. Recognize the Leader of the battle. God is the King of glory and victory. Psalm 24:8 says, "Who is this King of glory? The LORD strong and mighty, the LORD mighty in battle."

48. Remember that God helps us subdue our enemies. Psalm 47:2-3 says, "...he is a great King over all the earth. He shall subdue the people under us, and the nations under our feet."

49. Allow God to keep you in the place of victory. Psalm 55:22 says, "Cast thy burden upon the LORD, and he shall sustain thee: he shall never suffer the righteous to be moved."

50. Expect God to give you wisdom for the fight. James 1:5 says, "If any of you lack wisdom, let him ask of God,... and it shall be given him."

51. Remember that God battles with you against the enemy. Deuteronomy 20:4 says, "For the LORD your God is he that goeth with you, to fight for you against your enemies, to save you."

52. Ask God for spiritual strength. Isaiah 26:4-5 says, "Trust ye in the LORD for ever: for in the LORD JEHOVAH is everlasting strength...."

53. Remember God fights on your behalf. Nehemiah 4:20 says, "...our God shall fight for us."

54. Realize your battle is not for the kingdoms of this world. John 18:36 says, "Jesus answered, My kingdom is not of this world: if my kingdom were of this world, then would my servants fight...."

55. Be valiant in the fight. Hebrews 11:34 says, "...waxed valiant in fight, turned to flight the armies of the aliens."

56. Do not fear the dangers of battle. Psalms 91:5,7 says, "Thou shalt not be afraid for the terror by night; nor for the arrow that flieth by day;...it shall not come nigh thee."

57. Do not fear the power of the enemy. Joshua 10:25 says, "...Fear not, nor be dismayed, be strong and of good courage: for thus shall the LORD do to all your enemies against whom ye fight."

58. Ask God for the knowledge to fight well. Proverbs 20:18 says, "Every purpose is established by counsel: and with good advice make war."

Remember, the devil will be judged by God. The devil is no longer in God's favor. He chose to disobey God. God judges disobedience, having the authority to punish all evildoers. God has prepared a place of torment for the devil.

59. Recognize that Satan fell from an exalted position. Isaiah 14:12 says, "How art thou fallen from heaven, O Lucifer, son of the morning! how art thou cut down to the ground...."

60. Know that Satan willfully disobeyed God. Isaiah 14:13-14 says, "...I will ascend into heaven, I will exalt my throne above the stars of God...I will be like the most High."

61. Remember that God has a place of judgment prepared for Satan. Isaiah 14:15 says, "Yet thou shalt be brought down to hell, to the sides of the pit."

62. Realize that the devil knows his end. Revelation 20:10 says, "And the devil was cast into the lake of fire and brimstone,... and shall be tormented... for ever and ever."

63. Realize that the evil angels who followed the devil will share in his punishment. Jude 1:6 says, "And the angels which kept not their first estate, but left their own habitation, he hath reserved in everlasting chains under darkness unto the judgment of the great day."

Learn to stay in the place of victory through Jesus Christ. Jesus won the greatest battle against the devil when He gave His life willingly on the cross. Jesus gained back what man lost, and the devil was defeated for eternity.

64. Realize that you are seated in heavenly places. Ephesians 2:6 says, "And hath... made us sit together in heavenly places in Christ Jesus...."

65. Thank God for great victory. Ephesians 3:20 says, "Now unto him that is able to do exceeding abundantly above all that we ask or think, according to the power that worketh in us."

66. Know that you have the mind of Christ. First Corinthians 2:16 says, "...But we have the mind of Christ."

67. Realize that you have been rescued from darkness. Colossians 1:13 says, "Who hath delivered us from the power of darkness, and hath translated us into the kingdom of his dear Son...."

68. Remember that the light of God's Word reproves the devil. Ephesians 5:13 says, "But all things that are reproved are made manifest by the light...."

69. Hold on to God's promises. Second Peter 1:4 says, "Whereby are given unto us exceeding great and precious promises: that by these ye might be partakers of the divine nature, having escaped the corruption that is in the world through lust."

70. Believe that the Lord is exalted above the enemy. First Chronicles 29:11 says, "Thine, O LORD, is the greatness, and the power, and the glory, and the victory, and the majesty:...and thou art exalted as head above all."

71. Praise God that you are in His kingdom. Matthew 16:19 says, "And I will give unto thee the keys of the kingdom of heaven:...."

Enjoy God's rewards for faithfulness in the battle. God wants to give His warriors the spoils of victory. Sometimes you will have a part in winning souls for God's kingdom. Rejoice in God's favor.

72. Participate in every godly victory. First Samuel 30:24 says, "...his part is that goeth down to the battle, so shall his part be that tarrieth by the stuff: they shall part alike."

73. Possess what the enemy tried to keep. Deuteronomy 20:14 says, "...thou shalt eat the spoil of thine enemies, which the LORD thy God hath given thee."

74. Receive your heavenly reward. First Peter 1:4 says, "To an inheritance ...reserved in heaven for you...."

75. Receive an anointing from God. Psalms 23:5 says, "Thou preparest a table before me in the presence of mine enemies: thou anointest my head with oil; my cup runneth over."

Remember that God's hand protects your life. At times, the battle may seem so intense that you think all is lost. God's peace will be with you even on the most stressful occasions.

76. Believe you will have peace in the enemies' land. Deuteronomy 12:10 says, "...he giveth you rest from all your enemies round about, so that ye dwell in safety...."

77. Keep your peace in the middle of the battle. Psalm 55:18 says, "He hath delivered my soul in peace from the battle that was against me...."

78. Enjoy God's rest in the midst of the battle. Deuteronomy 12:10 says, "...your God giveth... you rest from all your enemies round about, so that ye dwell in safety...."

79. Do not be terrified by the circumstances. Deuteronomy 20:3-4 says, "...battle against your enemies: let not your hearts faint, fear not, and do not

tremble, neither be ye terrified because of them; For the LORD your God is he that goeth with you, to fight for you against your enemies, to save you."

80. Chase the enemy in the midst of his attack. Deuteronomy 28:7 says, "The LORD shall cause thine enemies that rise up against thee to be smitten before thy face: they shall come out against thee one way, and flee before thee seven ways."

81. Remember the Lord will pay back Satan for persecution of believers. Deuteronomy 30:7 says, "And the LORD thy God will put all these curses upon thine enemies, and on them that hate thee, which persecuted thee."

82. Realize your enemies cannot stand before God. Joshua 21:44, "And the LORD gave them rest round about,... and there stood not a man of all their enemies before them; the LORD delivered all their enemies into their hand."

83. Remember the devil cannot stand the presence of a faithful follower of God. James 4:7 says, "Submit yourselves therefore to God. Resist the devil, and he will flee from you."

Walk with God in all your ways. Don't wait for Satan to attack. Take positive steps to defeat his kingdom. Follow the Word of God and study His commands.

84. Listen for God's voice. Exodus 23:22 says, "But if thou shalt indeed obey his voice, and do all that I speak; then I will be an enemy unto thine enemies, and an adversary unto thine adversaries."

85. Walk in God's abundance. Deuteronomy 8:18 says, "But thou shalt remember the LORD thy God: for it is he that giveth thee power to get wealth...."

86. Claim your heritage that will keep you from the devil's destruction. Isaiah 54:17 says, "No weapon that is formed against thee shall prosper...."

Let Jesus save you from the devil's plans. The devil's plans are destructive, but God wants you to be the overcomer. Rely on God's plan and strength.

87. Praise Jesus for paying the penalty of sin. John 1:29 says, "...Behold the Lamb of God, which taketh away the sin of the world."

88. Realize that Jesus destroyed the power of death. Hebrews 2:14 says, "...he might destroy him that had the power of death, that is, the devil...."

89. Let Jesus help you destroy the works of the devil. First John 3:8 says, "...For this purpose the Son of God was manifested, that he might destroy the works of the devil."

90. Allow Jesus' blood to speak victory for you. Revelation 12:11 says, "And they overcame him by the blood of the Lamb, and by the word of their testimony...."

91. Remember God's love for you is greater than the enemy's hatred. John 3:16 says, "For God so loved the world, that he gave his only begotten Son...."

92. Let Jesus complete what is lacking in you. Colossians 2:10 says, "And ye are complete in him, which is the head of all principality and power."

93. See Christ as the life in you. Colossians 3:4 says, "When Christ, who is our life, shall appear, then shall ye also appear with him in glory."

Learn the powerful ways God has given you to fight the devil. As spiritual warfare increases, God will direct you by His Word. God has given offensive and defensive weapons to His army. Use them wisely.

94. Win through love and prayer. Matthew 5:44 says, "... Love your enemies, bless them that curse you, do good to them that hate you, and pray for them..."

95. Minister grace to others. Ephesians 4:29 says, "Let no corrupt communication proceed out of your mouth, but that which is good to the use of edifying, that it may minister grace unto the hearers."

96. Fight a fight of faith. First Timothy 6:12 says, "Fight the good fight of faith, lay hold on eternal life, whereunto thou art also called...."

97. Take your thoughts captive to God's will. Second Corinthians 10:5 says, "Casting down imaginations, and every high thing that exalteth itself against the knowledge of God, and bringing into captivity every thought to the obedience of Christ."

98. Have faith in the Word of God, which is Truth. John 17:17 says, "Sanctify them through thy truth: thy word is truth."

99. Thank God for His wonderful works. First Thessalonians 2:13 says, "...ye received ...as it is in truth, the word of God, which effectually worketh also in you that believe."

100. Avoid devilish traps that appear to be good things. Second Timothy 2:22 says, "Flee also youthful lusts: but follow righteousness, faith, charity, peace...."

101. Stay attached to the Branch of might. Colossians 2:7 says, "Rooted and built up in him, and stablished in the faith...."

Scriptures of Victory

Look up and read these Scriptures. Repeat them, and let them become part of your arsenal. God will lead you to total victory.

Isaiah 60:2	Psalms 118:11-16
Psalms 121:5-8	Psalms 124:8
Revelation 3:10	Colossians 3:10

Finally, my brethren, be strong in the Lord, and in the power of his might. Put on the whole armour of God, that ye may be able to stand against the wiles of the devil. For we wrestle not against flesh and blood, but against principalities, against powers, against the rulers of the darkness of this world, against spiritual wickedness in high places. Wherefore take unto you the whole armour of God, that ye may be able to withstand in the evil day, and having done all, to stand.

Ephesians 6:10-13.

Endnotes

Chapter 1

1. Brown, Driver, Briggs and Gesenius, *The KJV Old Testament Hebrew Lexicon,* "Hebrew Lexicon entry for Heylel," S.V. "Lucifer," Isaiah 14:12. Available from <http://www.biblestudytools.nct/Lexicons/Hebrew/heb.cgi?number=1966&version=kjv>.

2. Thayer and Smith, *The KJV New Testament Greek Lexicon,* "Greek Lexicon entry for Diabolos," S.V. "devil," Revelation 12:9. Available from <http://www.biblestudytools.net/Lexicons/Greek/grk.cgi?number=1228&version=kjv>.

3. Thayer and Smith, "Greek Lexicon entry for Abaddon," S.V. Abaddon," Revelation 9:11. Available from <http://www.biblestudytools.net/Lexicons/Greek/grk.cgi?number=3&version=kjv>.

4. Ibid., "Greek Lexicon entry for Apolluon," S.V. Apollyon," Revelation 9:11. Available from <http://www.biblestudytools.net/Lexicons/Greek/grk.cgi?number=623&version=kjv>.

5. Based on a definition from *Merriam-Webster's Collegiate Dictionary,* 11th ed. (Springfield, Massechusetts: Merriam-Webster, Inc., 2003), S.V. "Beelzebub."

Chapter 4

1. Based on a definition from Brown, Driver, Briggs and Gesenius, "Hebrew Lexicon entry for Kabash," available from <http://www.biblestudytools.net/Lexicons/Hebrew/heb.cgi?number=3533&version=kjv>.

Chapter 5

1. Based on a definition from *Merriam-Webster's,* S.V. "unction."

2. Based on a definition from Brown, Driver, Briggs and Gesenius, "Hebrew Lexicon entry for Nuwc," S.V. "standard," Isaiah 51:19. Available from <http://www.biblestudytools.net/Lexicons/Hebrew/heb.cgi?number=5127&version=kjv>.

Chapter 6

1. Brown, Driver, Briggs and Gesenius, "Hebrew Lexicon entry for Barak," S.V. "blessed," Genesis 1:28. Available from <http://www.biblestudytools.net/Lexicons/Hebrew/heb.cgi?number=1288&version=kjv>.

2. Based on a definition from *Merriam-Webster's,* S.V. "bless."

Chapter 7

1. Thayer and Smith, "Greek Lexicon entry for Dunamis," S.V. "power," Acts 1:8. Available from <http://www.biblestudytools.net/Lexicons/Greek/grk.cgi?number=1411&version=kjv>.

2. Based on a definition from Thayer and Smith, "Greek Lexicon entry for Exousia," S.V. "power," Luke 10:19. Available from <http://www.biblestudytools.net/Lexicons/Greek/grk.cgi?number=1849&version=kjv>.

Chapter 8

1. Brown, Driver, Briggs and Gesenius, "Hebrew Lexicon entry for elyown," S.V. "high," Genesis 14:19. Available from <http://www.biblestudytools.net/Lexicons/Hebrew/heb.cgi?number=5945&version=kjv>.

Chapter 10

1. Brown, Driver, Briggs and Gesenius, "Hebrew Lexicon entry for Towb," S.V. "goodly," Exodus 2:2. Available from <http://www.biblestudytools.net/Lexicons/Hebrew/heb.cgi?number=2896&version=kjv>.

2. Ibid., "Hebrew Lexicon entry for Mosheh, S.V. "Moses," Genesis 2:10. Available from <http://www.biblestudytools.net/Lexicons/Hebrew/heb.cgi?number=4872&version=kjv>.

Chapter 11

1. Thayer and Smith, "Greek Lexicon entry for Ekballo," S.V. "cast out," Mark 6:13; 11:15. Available from<http://www.biblestudytools.net/Lexicons/Greek/grk.cgi?number=1544&version=kjv>.

2. Brown, Driver, Briggs and Gesenius, "Hebrew Lexicon entry for Yada," S.V. "know," Exodus 33:15. Available from <http://www.biblestudytools.net/Lexicons/Hebrew/heb.cgi?number=3045&version=kjv>.